THE FABERGÉ CASE

FROM THE PRIVATE COLLECTION OF JOHN TRAINA

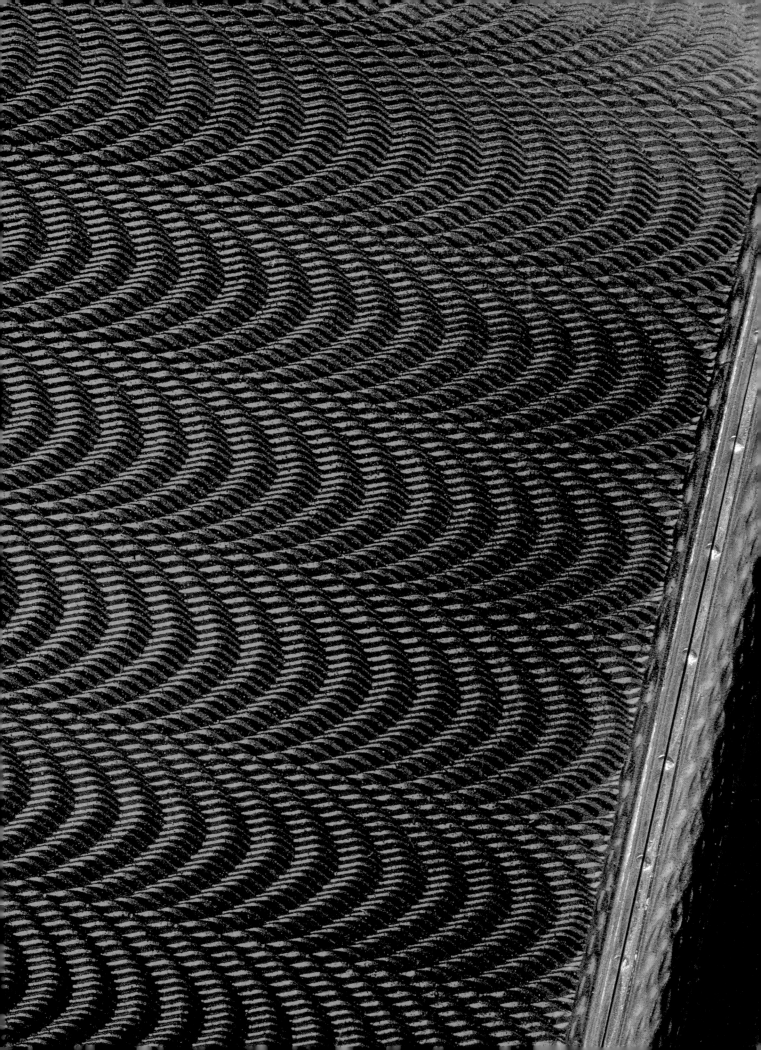

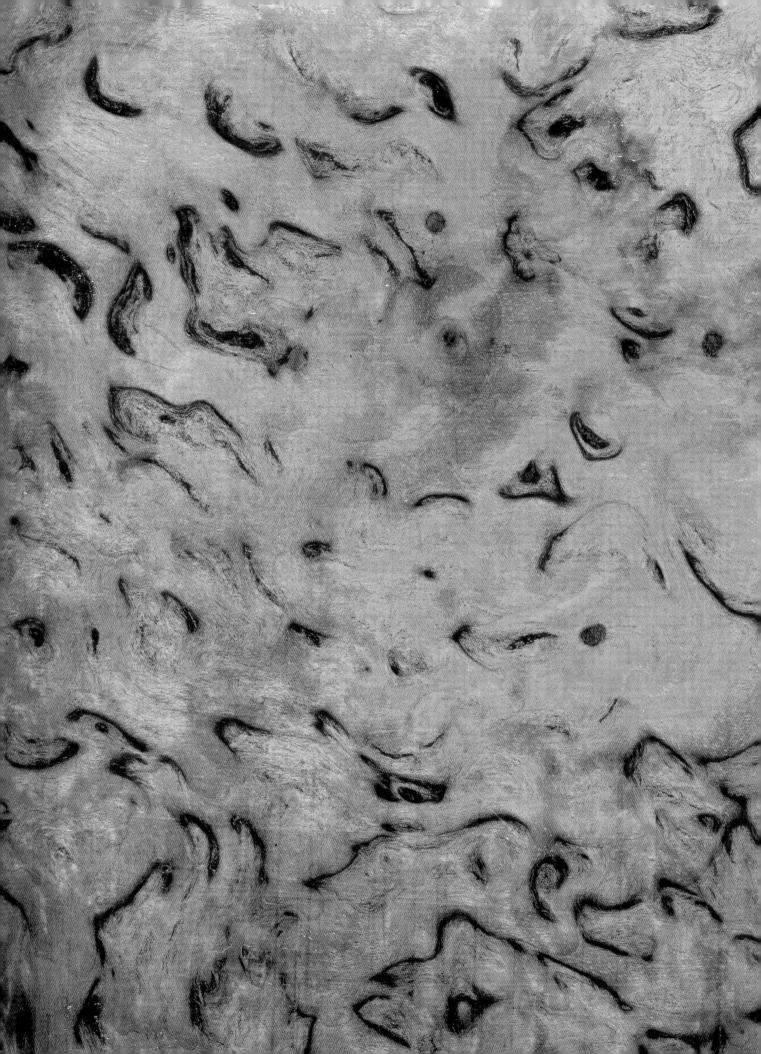

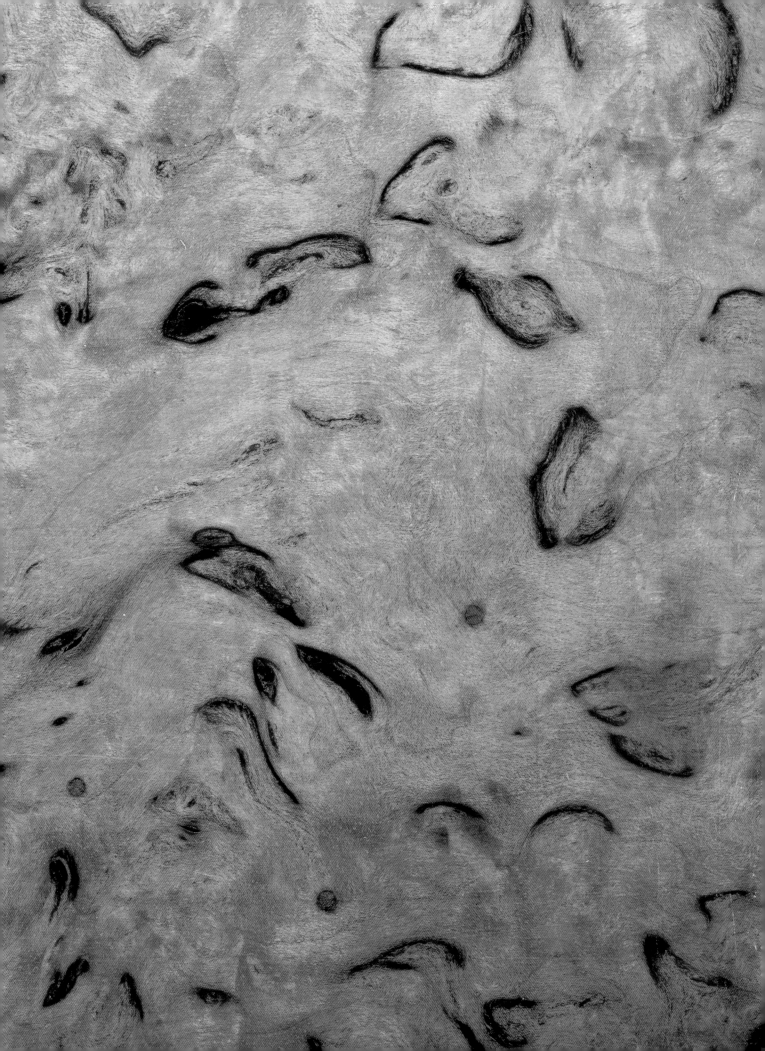

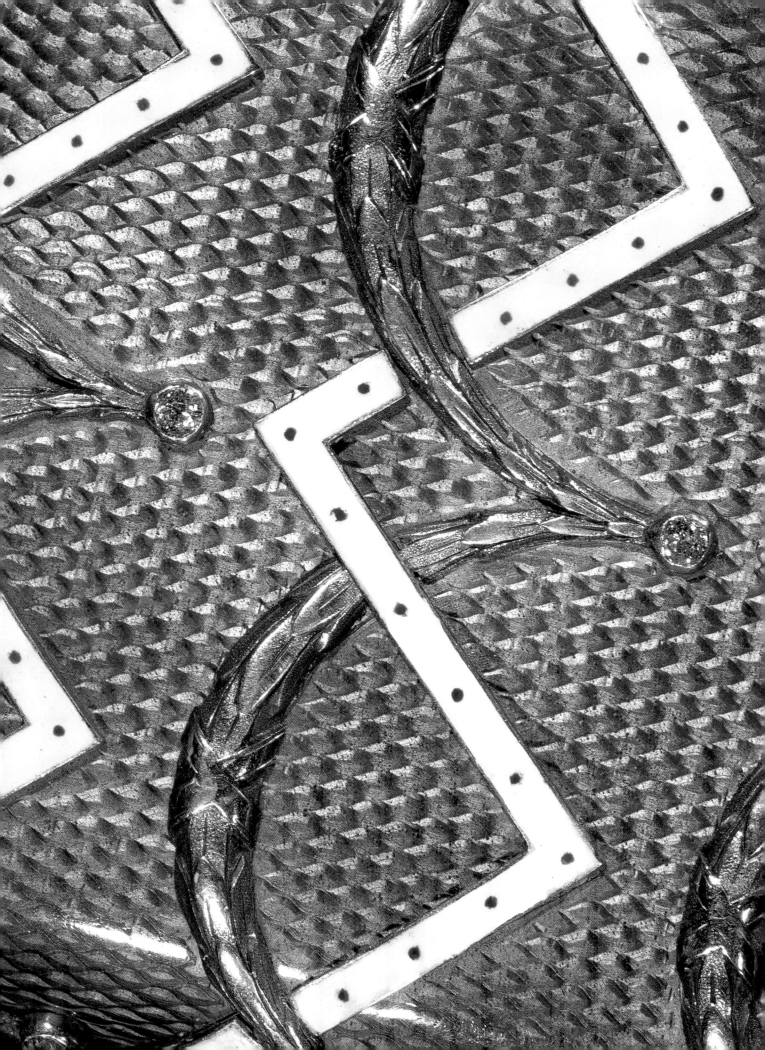

THE FABERGÉ CASE

FROM THE PRIVATE COLLECTION OF JOHN TRAINA

BY JOHN TRAINA

PHOTOGRAPHS BY FRED LYON
FOREWORD BY MIKHAIL PIOTROVSKY
INTRODUCTION BY ARCHDUKE GÉZA VON HABSBURG
ESSAY BY DANIELLE STEEL

HARRY N. ABRAMS, INC., PUBLISHERS

Editors: SHARON AVRUTICK and AMY L. VINCHESI
Designer: DIRK LUYKX

Library of Congress Cataloging-in-Publication Data
Fabergé, Peter Carl, 1846–1920.
The Fabergé case : from the private collection of John Traina /
photographs by Fred Lyon ; foreword by Mikhail Piotrovsky ;
introduction by Archduke Géza von Habsburg ; essay by Danielle Steel.
p.   cm.
Includes bibliographical references and index.
ISBN 0–8109–3344–6 (hardcover)
1. Fabergé (Firm)—Catalogs. 2. Fabergé, Peter Carl, 1846–1920—
Catalogs. 3. Cigarette cases—Russia (Federation)—Catalogs.
4. Cigarette cases—Private collections—California—San Francisco—
Catalogs. 5. Traina, John—Art collections—Catalogs. I. Lyon,
Fred. II. Steel, Danielle. III. Title.
NK7398.F33A4 1998
739.2'092—dc21   98–4215

Published in 1998 by Harry N. Abrams, Incorporated, New York

Printed and bound in Hong Kong

Harry N. Abrams, Inc.
100 Fifth Avenue
New York, N.Y. 10011
www.abramsbooks.com

CONTENTS

A Case for Fabergé

By Dr. Mikhail Piotrovsky
Director, The State Hermitage Museum

FABERGÉ is a symbol: a symbol of all things Russian—history, heritage, culture, and icons, as well as the glorious old St. Petersburg of which we all dream.

With profound nostalgia, the work of Fabergé evokes a Russia laden with cultural landmarks that are among history's greatest. From 1918, after the Russian Revolution, Fabergé's works became a famous symbol of all things gone. Gone were the days of a society hearing for the first time Tchaikovsky's *Swan Lake*, *The Nutcracker*, and *Sleeping Beauty*; or reading Tolstoy's *Anna Karenina* and the works of Chekhov and Dostoyevsky. Each Fabergé piece bears quiet witness to the fascinating stories connected to the lives of its owners, givers, and recipients; to the people who lived with the pieces, used them, displayed them, and collected them for their beauty, value, and function. Czars, Empresses, Grand Dukes, Dukes, Queens, and Princes were among those coveting these treasures, as were military leaders and wealthy Westerners well versed in the elegant symbols of a great culture.

The works of Fabergé did not merely emulate their surroundings. They led the way; the Fabergé style, the pinnacle of Russian achievement, was followed by all other Russian art. His work was also a part of Russian history. The stable of Fabergé workmasters worked together, like an architectural team, each one contributing a building block to make the whole, which, once complete, embodied his unique spirit. The works of Fabergé became known as "Russian International Style," incorporating Japanese, Chinese, Indian, Renaissance, Empire, Gothic, Persian, Louis XV and XVI styles, and Greek, to name a few. Fabergé, himself of Huguenot descent, employed workmasters from around the world. None were there to practice their native country's style of art; all were "Russianized" enough to create something that would marry craftsmanship with beauty and Russian symbols. Fabergé is symbolic of foreigners coming and Russians leaving, a symbol bringing knowledge of Russian style to the world. There is a Fabergé circle, and in the story of Fabergé is the story of Russian emigration.

But how did the pieces, the cigarette cases themselves, emigrate to tell this story? How could these sometimes fragile works of art safely reach their destinations, given the

Silver-gilt cigarette case decorated with golden-yellow translucent enamel over sunburst *guilloché* design emanating from the center of the case, which is mounted with a rose-cut diamond. Unusual flip-over gold-chased clasp.
Initials of HENRIK WIGSTRÖM. St. Petersburg 1908–17. 4⅛″. Exhibition: Shown at Neiman Marcus for the San Francisco Fine Arts Museums

traveling conditions of the times? How did these masterpieces go undetected at the borders?

I believe that Fabergé's cigarette cases were the most portable of the Fabergé objects. Since they were small, they could be easily transported unnoticed across borders, as many of them were. A gentleman, even a refugee gentleman, needed his cigarettes, especially on a journey, and what better, more elegant way to travel than with a case by Fabergé? And even if they were found, since they were considered to be personal necessities, the cases were unlikely to be confiscated. Thus these pieces were ideally suited to experience the life and times of St. Petersburg and then carry those stories to all points of the world—to convey to the world the stories of Russia and of Fabergé, as Russian émigrés and their cases settled in Paris, Germany, elsewhere throughout Europe, the Far East, and America.

The greatest variety of Fabergé's art is visible in the cases. Although they range widely in design, colors, textures, themes, and materials, they share common features of elegance and impeccable craftsmanship including perfectly fitting lids and invisible hinges. I should emphasize that one must experience the tactile sense of the boxes to understand and appreciate them fully. The diversity of materials used includes silver, gold, enamel, gunmetal, stones, and wood in countless combinations, as well as inlaid inscriptions, decorations, rose-cut diamonds, and cabochon sapphires. Many cases were made in homage to Russian icons, some told a story—a private joke perhaps—and others referred to significant years, animals, or holidays. The variety is endless.

Today, many Fabergé cigarette cases are housed in museums, including the Hermitage. But they are also featured in private collections of treasures and in exclusive auction houses as well—with much lauding of the provenance and rich history associated with Fabergé. These representatives of Russia continue to keep alive the story of the imperial jeweler, Peter Carl Fabergé, his much-loved St. Petersburg, and the grand Russia that was.

INTRODUCTION

Fabergé's Cigarette Cases

By Dr. Géza von Habsburg

ABERGÉ specialists are always somewhat at a loss—albeit no longer entirely surprised—to explain the never-ceasing fascination of the general public with the objects of art, jewels, and silver artifacts of this master *bijoutier*. Anyone who visited the exhibition "Fabergé in America" at the Metropolitan Museum of Art in New York on one of the weekends in March 1996, when the number of daily visitors topped ten thousand, may be interested to learn that in that year this exhibition ranked fourth worldwide in average daily attendance—sandwiched between Philadelphia's "Cézanne" and Madrid's "Goya"—flanked therefore by the world's greatest post-Impressionist artist and the most popular of Spanish old masters. The more than $5 million paid recently for one of Fabergé's Easter eggs underscores the extraordinary reappraisal of the Russian jeweler-craftsman that has taken place within the last twenty years. Considered in the 1930s and '40s to be "secondhand" baubles, his objects of art have risen to stardom, easily outclassing the work of his competitors, whom Fabergé in 1904 labeled as "people of commerce," as opposed to artist-jewelers, an exclusive category in which he included himself and perhaps René Lalique.

It is nevertheless with mixed feelings that a Fabergé fan might greet the spawning of yet another study on this master craftsman, to be added to over forty existing monographs/catalogues and the more than two thousand entries computed today by Fabergé's bibliographers. Yet, as the reader will see, the present offering fills an interesting gap in our knowledge.

Collectors of yesteryear aspired to render homage to Fabergé by presenting as complete a picture as possible of the master's creations, acquiring specimens of all types of works of art produced by his firm. Today, the trend is to specialize. We now have, for instance, one collector who will buy only Fabergé perfume bottles. Another will disdain everything except Fabergé clocks. These are easily outstripped by John Traina of San Francisco, who has spent the last twenty years amassing what is the world's largest collection of Russian cigarette cases, thus earning himself the title "King of the Fabergé Cigarette Case."

What might at first seem a mundane exercise—namely that of hoarding what are mostly flat, rectangular receptacles for cigarettes—in fact ends up as one of the most fascinating and rewarding studies of Fabergé's versatility. His hundreds of renderings of a basic theme are a distant echo of such geniuses of the variation as Bach or Liszt. King Edward VII's well-known dictum to Fabergé comes to mind: "Let us have no duplicates!" and is clearly borne out by the apparently never-ending stream—yea, torrent!—of novel designs that issued from the St. Petersburg and Moscow workshops.

The widespread passion for tobacco in one form or another bore a stigma as early as 1599, when its effect was described as: "Mortifieth and bennumeth: Causeth drowsinesse: troubleth and dulleth the scences: makes (as it were) drunke: dangerous in meale time." In 1604 King James I critcized the use of tobacco as: "loathsome to the eye, hatefull to the nose, harmefull to the braine, dangerous to the lungs."[1] (Our surgeon general might find such passages entertaining and consoling reading material.) In the eighteenth century the taking of snuff was indulged by all and sundry. This included the ladies of the New World, who avidly emulated their French counterparts to an extent that they were warned against the use of "ye Irreverent practice of taking Snuff, or handing Snuff boxes one to another in Meetings."[2]

To this dangerous habit we owe the exquisite microcosmos of the eighteenth-century snuffbox. Jewel-set examples were presented by French kings as tokens of royal favor to visiting monarchs and ambassadors throughout the eighteenth century. Such avid takers of snuff as Count Heinrich von Bruhl, Prime Minister of Saxony, and King Frederick the Great of Prussia are both said to have possessed collections of three hundred snuffboxes, almost one for every day of the year. By 1800 the taking of snuff was gradually being replaced by the new vogue of "smoaking." Yet the royal tradition of presenting snuffboxes continued, until World War I set an end to such an antiquated custom. Fabergé's glamorous imperial presentation snuffboxes are the last significant examples of this genre soon to be replaced by the cigarette case.

Following the Crimean War (1853–56) the cigarette rapidly gained ascendance over all other forms of tobacco consumption. Much as with the 1950s films of Humphrey Bogart, visualizing the early 1900s era of Edward, Prince of Wales (later King of England); his son King George V; and his cousins, Nicholas, the young Czar of Russia, and Wilhelm, the German Kaiser, is unthinkable without the compulsory appendix of a cigarette. The art of the cigarette case flourished worldwide. Examples in gold applied with the jewel-set ciphers of the monarchs of Austria, Bulgaria, Germany, and Great Britain, to mention only the most common, make their appearance toward 1900. The thousands of Russian silver cigarette cases that have survived—only a fraction of those actually made—are a testimony to this epidemic, which has lasted up to the present. From the 1880s on, the cigarette case applied with a diamond-set crown, monogram, cipher, or miniature became the gift the Czar presented most frequently on numerous trips abroad, as well as in Russia to visiting diplomats.

As early as 1885 the archives of the imperial Cabinet mention a first payment of 252 rubles to Fabergé for a "cigarette case with a sapphire and rose-cut diamond pansy," which Their Imperial Majesties took on a trip to Copenhagen.[3] This is followed by a silver cigarette case with gold arms costing 75 rubles. Two years later a payment of 501 rubles was made to Fabergé "for additional roses, gold, and silver and for the design of twenty-four(!) cigarette cases." In 1891, on the occasion of the voyage to the Far East by the Czarevich Nicholas on board the cruiser *Pamiat Azova*, eight diamond-set snuffboxes were ordered for prices up to 1,850 rubles, along with five silver cigarette cases with gold double-headed eagles set with sapphires costing between 87 and 160 rubles; a further twelve silver cases were added three months later (45 to 80 rubles). While the expensive snuffboxes were obviously intended as gifts to high-ranking dignitaries, the cheaper cigarette cases were destined for the less privileged. Soon after this time, snuffboxes virtually disappear from among the orders of the imperial Cabinet. Thus, for example, for the coronation of Nicholas II in 1896, the imperial Cabinet ordered twelve enamel cigarette cases in groups of four, each costing between 500 and 700 rubles.

Sadly, the invoices for imperial commissions seem to have survived only incompletely. Thus there is no mention of what must have been the ultimate cigarette case, ordered by Nicholas II as a fiftieth birthday present for his uncle, Grand Duke Nikolai Nikolaievich (November 18, 1918): a platinum case weighing a full pound emblazoned with the Czar's diamond-set cipher and applied with jeweled double-headed eagles at each corner. It was estimated by Fabergé's staff at 50,000 rubles, twice the cost of the firm's most expensive imperial Easter egg![4]

Fabergé's cigarette cases offer a perfect opportunity to scrutinize all the varied forms of this master's craftsmanship. Superlative and imaginative engine turning, seamless soldering, and painstaking chasing of metals are the signatures of the master's gold and silver workshops. Carefully handcrafted borders are tooled with bands of laurel or palm leaves. Openwork applications of rococo scrolls (see pp. 73 and 109), double-headed eagles, emblems, and other motifs are often applied to the covers, attached by pins and telltale domed nuts; many such examples can be seen in the Traina Collection. Well-nigh invisible hinges and tight-fitting covers, closing almost hermetically, are Fabergé's trademarks.

The inimitable quality of Fabergé's carving is visible, time and time again, in the often wafer-thin walls of the cases created from carefully selected hardstones. Most frequently they are carved from a rare translucent spinach-colored nephrite (see p. 115). Access to this high-quality mineral was apparently reserved exclusively for Fabergé's collaborator Karl Woerffel. A large block of this nephrite stood in the courtyard of Fabergé's house at 24 Bolshaya Morskaya, from which Woerffel could chip off suitable chunks. Less often, Fabergé's workshops used bloodstone, agate, bowenite, and, most rarely, rhodonite and rock crystal. In all cases the edges are beautifully beveled or perfectly rounded in a manner that hardstone carvers at Idar-Oberstein in Germany, and forgers worldwide, find impossible to replicate today.

Fabergé's legendary stature as an enameler, too, is triumphantly displayed in his cigarette cases. Enameling in the round (*en ronde bosse*) was developed by French crafts-men in the 1760s, best visible in the snuffboxes they made for the Parisian court. The Swiss in Geneva closely followed in their footsteps. Fabergé and his master craftsmen, in particular the brilliant Michael Perchin, studied the technique of such objects of art among the many originals in the jewelry gallery of the Hermitage. Beginning in 1884[5] the first rudimentary essays in enameling were undertaken. By 1887, the year of the blue Serpent Clock egg, the firm had mastered the skill of producing opalescent enamels. From then on, Fabergé's craftsmen developed, over successive years, by trial and error, a palette said to have offered a choice of 145 hues. By comparison, Fabergé's competitors, such as Carl Hahn, Alexander Tillander, and Ivan Britzin, kept to a small number of relatively "safe" colors—white, pale and dark blue, scarlet, pink, yellow, and green. Fabergé created such exceptional hues as, for instance, luscious emerald green, deep rich plum, steel gray, and lime green, all of which were no doubt exceedingly difficult to achieve (and to repli-cate), as they appear in only a handful of objects. Some of these colors can be seen in the Traina Collection. Fabergé's unique, flawless, and glossy enamels were the fruit of weeks and months of laborious work.

All styles, both historical and innovative, are represented in the art of the ciga-rette case. With total ease and familiarity, Fabergé was able to use the idiom of each and every French style—all the Louis, as well as Empire and "Retour d'Égypte." Art Nouveau, a movement that Fabergé spearheaded in Russia, appears in his oeuvre by 1898 and remained a favorite among his Moscow clientele (see pp. 124–25). Finally, there are cases that in their geometric simplicity seem to herald Art Deco (see pp. 54, 99, 145). But in the end the most memorable of Fabergé's inventions is the classic ribbed gold case with a single cabochon thumbpiece, of which many variations exist (see p. 126). This simple, yet so distinguished design, which we take for granted today, remains the most lasting legacy of the great Russian master.

The John Traina Collection of Fabergé cigarette cases is a unique example of the total devotion of one man—a nonsmoker!—to an eminently deserving subject. Together with the miniature Easter eggs, cigarette cases were the most popular article sold by Fabergé. Once, many thousands must have existed. The presentation in this book of over three hundred examples of cigarette cases by Fabergé and his contemporaries permits an exciting insight into the genius of one man, one family, one firm.

[1] Henry Buttes, *Dyets Dry Dinner*, 1599. Quoted from Claire le Corbeiller, *European and American Snuff Boxes 1730–1830*, Viking Press, 1966, p. 2.
[2] James I, *Counterblaste to tobacco*, 1604. *Ibid.*
[3] Around 1900 and until the eve of World War I, the ruble was worth approximately 50 cents. The author wishes to thank Marina Lopato, Curator of Western Applied Art at the Hermitage Museum, for access to transcripts of the files of the imperial Cabinet.

[4] Ulla Tillander, "New Light on the Workshop of Henrik Wigström," in *Fabergé: Imperial Jeweller* (St. Petersburg/Paris/London catalogue 1993–94), Abrams, 1994, p. 102.
[5] Snuffbox presented by Czar Alexander III to Reichskanzler Bismarck in 1884. Collection Princes of Bismarck, Germany. See Géza von Habsburg, *Fabergé* (Munich exhibition catalogue 1986–87), Vendome Press, 1988, cat. no. 404.

On Collecting

BY JOHN TRAINA

THE IDEA that Fabergé cases were items designed to be *used* appealed to me far more than if they had been intended simply to be *collected*.

As H. C. Bainbridge so aptly describes cigarette cases in *Peter Carl Fabergé*:

They serve a useful purpose, and as constant companions endear themselves to the possessor, they are pleasing to look at and pleasant to feel, and above all have in them that quality I have called "substance" which creates that sense of well-being which I believe to be the main reason for the attraction of all Fabergé objects.

I buy Fabergé to use it and collect pieces of Fabergé that are functional. It has been recorded that even Malcolm Forbes used many of his Fabergé items in his office—including a pencil holder, a couple of bell pushes, a calendar, and, of course, a cigarette case—on a daily basis. Czar Nicholas II, too, collected cigarette cases for his daily use.

A cigarette case carried in an inside pocket, handled, presented, and used, was what was most appealing to me from the start, and it still is. And the cases are available in such a tremendous variety of shapes, colors, sizes, and material, all rendered with such history attached that each one was a special addition to the collection.

Because cigarette cases have been fascinating to me, I have chosen to feature them in this book to show the reader this particular part of the world of Fabergé's art. By the time I started acquiring—long after the end of the 1917 Russian Revolution and long after Fabergé had stopped producing art and objects for sale—his work had become desirable as a collectible. Some other fine pieces of Fabergé art were collected in his own time: jewels (by almost all who could afford them), exquisite stone figures and statuettes, jeweled eggs, imperial Easter eggs (special gifts commissioned by the Czar, his family, and royal families of Europe), enamels, picture frames, clocks, and so on. The Queen of

England preferred finely carved animals, as did the Dowager Empress of Russia; there were gem and hardstone flowers for the Czarina; and in many of the royal palaces of Europe and as far away as Siam, elaborate pieces of silver, gold, and gems decorated the halls and tables.

What interests me the most historically was that a useful, yet beautiful, cigarette case was probably always in the royal pocket or purse. It was a daily accoutrement intended for regular use, and it always traveled with its owner. This explains the importance of the touch and feel of each piece; its size, shape, and material were selected to give pleasure before, during, and after its actual use. The flat surfaces of the cases also allowed the workmasters to express their special art and talent.

As smoking was quite fashionable in turn-of-the-century Russia, so were the cases. They were popular gifts, given on birthdays, anniversaries, religious holidays (especially Christmas and Easter), state holidays, retirements, military victories, and numerous commemorative occasions—even as an amusing reminder of a night of debauchery or a hunting expedition.

The Imperial Court in St. Petersburg kept an inventory of up to four thousand cases for the Czar, court officials, military officers, and the imperial family to hand out at such occasions. The Czar took cases along on his travels to foreign courts to present to leaders, diplomats, military officers, local officials, and friends. And then there was his ample supply for personal and family use. (They all smoked at that time—it was even encouraged.) The cases traveled easily then, as they do now, spreading the word of Fabergé to other royal courts around the world. Though the majority of Fabergé's pieces were in Russia and Europe in his day, America is now where most of them reside.

The great wealth of the Romanoffs—the world's most wealthy leaders—along with the rich resources of Russia has long intrigued buyers, as can be seen during any auction sale of such pieces. The search for a case for sale also is fascinating. Surprise finds in flea markets in Russia and France, antique shops, the wares of traveling salesmen, and small shops add to the excitement of the treasure hunt.

For me, collecting the cases is only half the fun. Researching each piece is of particular interest to me—I love to investigate the styles of the makers, the pieces' marks, hallmarks, export marks, or lack of marks, all of which add to my curiosity. Even the scratches, bumps, and dents tell a story. Inscriptions, signatures, dates, crests, initials, military use, military rank, ships, travels, wars, Easter, love, and fun are all recorded in symbols, signs, sayings, and code available to those who study them. Many inscriptions can be seen on the souvenir cases and require only imagination to understand.

Cigarette cases, more than other objects, express the art, use, and trends of the time. Many interesting and beautiful books exist covering the Fabergé eggs and decorative art. But I, and many others, agree with H. C. Bainbridge when he says: "To give a really representative display of these cigarette cases would call for a volume solely devoted to them because each one is different."

This book explores the case.

A Special Word About the Author

By Danielle Steel

WHEN ASKED to write about John Traina's book, I was told to speak candidly about living with a collector. And as he and I have not lived together for a number of years at this writing, I could have said somewhat tongue in cheek that the situation speaks for itself. But I did live with the collector, and the collection, for nearly two decades before that, so I do indeed have some experience with the subject.

Collecting is a fascinating thing. It is a kind of madness, a delicious obsession, an irresistible passion to those afflicted with it. John Traina is the consummate collector. He collects beautiful things. He collects objects—large and small, important and not, infinitely valuable, and thoroughly amusing. To say he collects everything would be unfair, but he has some very intriguing collections. Old cars, South Pacific art, antique wagons, ivory objects, malachite, tortoiseshell objects, military paraphernalia (cannons, insignia, and the like), and stuffed animals (one of my least favorite of his collections, it includes a fourteen-foot stuffed, once-live alligator, which—mea culpa—I once gave him for Valentine's Day, and a table whose four legs once belonged to a zebra). He collects antiques, certain kinds of art, maritime collectibles (everything from paintings to sailors' valentines—beautiful mementos made of tiny seashells), narwhal tusks, Japanese art, and, of course, Fabergé, mostly cigarette cases and animals.

What is collecting? It is, or must be, a passion to acquire, to have, to own, to see and admire, and sometimes, but not always, to use rare and wonderful and unique things—and to have as many of them as possible. If to have one such item is a great gift, to have five is more so, to have twenty is exciting, to have a hundred is sheer passion. The collection is the life force of the collector. The acquisition is part of it: the finding, the unearthing, the discovering, and the pursuing. Then the bartering, or winning at auction, sometimes at whatever price, or better yet at a bargain. And then the having, the shining, the polishing, the restoring, and finally the displaying and the owning. It is a kind of love for beautiful things. Many of them. Perhaps the ultimate collection in our case was our "collection" of nine beautiful children. More than most people would even think of. It was a passion we shared, more than all the others.

And next to the children, of course, perhaps John's handsomest collection is the Fabergé. It is extraordinary. Beautiful, varied, the largest of its kind, thorough, exquisite, extensive, rare. It is dazzling. And incredibly impressive.

And I think it may have been I who started this particular collection, with a gift I gave him shortly after we were married. It was a samorodok gold Fabergé case I found in the antique department at Cartier. Samorodok looks like ruffled gold that has been somehow swirled before it solidified to create an odd wavy surface, almost like finger painting in gold. It has an unusual and exotic look to it. Even today, the samorodok pieces remain among my favorite.

A little pink stone Fabergé pig, with diamond eyes, followed shortly after. And then another cigarette case. And with that, John was off and running. A series of beautiful gold cigarette cases ensued, and then at last a splendid enamel. And then another, and more, in a rainbow of exotic colors. Red, royal blue, pale blue, emerald green, mint green, a host of pinks, white, and yellow. And on to other materials, everything from gunmetal to copper to birchwood, rock crystal, agate, and nephrite. The possibilities were endless. And so the collection grew and grew and grew, and John's passion and expertise along with it. I think it's reasonable to assume by now that he is one of the most knowledgeable connoisseurs on the subject, and is often consulted by dealers and aficionados to attest to the authenticity of a case or simply acknowledge its beauty.

The collection he has now, that was once ours, is one of vast proportions, breathtaking scope, and startling richness. And along with the cases come myriad intriguing and often romantic stories. For me, they conjure up a lost world, the magic of imperial Russia, and it is easy to imagine handsome princes and dazzling generals bestowing them upon ladies, or even friends, as tokens of their esteem, or prizes of more clandestine, exotic moments. They were given to military men, courtesans, grandmothers, and royals, most often to commemorate a special occasion. And they appeared, nestled in velvet or satin, in handsome, specially made wooden boxes.

Among the many things that always intrigued me were the inscriptions. There is a particularly brilliant green oval one, which was given by both the Czar and Czarina on the occasion of the engagement of the Crown Prince Wilhelm of Sweden and Grand Duchess Maria Pavlovna. I gave it to John when our son Maxx was born, and he loved it. And there is one that never fails to bring tears to my eyes. It is a pale mint green with a diamond four-leaf clover on it, and the inscription reads simply: "To Nicky, love, Mama" (see pp. 36 and 50). It was a gift to the Czar from his mother. Perhaps it touches me because I also had a son named Nicky, who died tragically at age nineteen, and had I been part of that lost and nearly forgotten world of opulence and aristocratic glamour, perhaps I might have given *him* such a box during his life, with similar inscription. It is the only one of these many cases, that, because of my son, I would long to have.

These cases were not merely gifts to Czars, but exchanged between even slightly more ordinary people. They were highly prized, but not nearly as rare as they are now, though surely they must have been just as loved, and viewed as almost as precious as they are today.

Another kind that always intrigued me were the "souvenir cases." Usually made for military men, they are silver or gold, and attached to them are a collection of tiny ornaments and charms, scattered on the surface of the box, and representative of an entire lifetime. There are tiny miniatures of epaulets and military insignia, favorite animals, and little enamel bottles of champagne, and they are covered with engraved words and meaningful inscriptions. They always seem so personal to me and cannot help but make one dream of the people for whom they were made.

More recently, there are cases that passed through famous hands, like the one given to Cary Grant by Barbara Hutton, or those once owned by Frank Sinatra. They too have their own kind of magic, and make one stare at them, thinking, "Wow! Cary Grant *owned that* . . . he had it in his pocket. . . ."

There is another inscription I particularly love, almost as much as the one to the Czar from his mother. It is on a box which I now own. This one is probably the most romantic, and is written in French, rather than Cyrillic characters, which I cannot decipher. It is a relatively simple, small gold case, probably meant for a lady, and the neatly engraved handwriting inside says, "I would like to be a cigarette, to be lit the moment I touch your lips, and extinguished the moment I leave them." Who could possibly even dream of saying anything so romantic? How fitting that it should be on a case made by Carl Fabergé. It seems somehow perfect. Imagine for an instant . . . just imagine . . . close your eyes . . . and imagine receiving a gift like that one. Think what she must have felt when she saw it. I hope they loved each other deeply. I hope she appreciated what he said to her, and the gift he gave her, and the sentiment behind it.

For myself, I also like the cases in more unusual metals. I have always been particularly fascinated by the gunmetals, which seem kind of reversely chic and elegantly unpretentious. There is a half-leather, half-gold one I think very handsome. Some copper ones that have a rustic beauty. Some wooden ones that are very lovely. In some ways, they excite me more than the enamels, which are so obviously splendid. It is easy to catch the eye with precious stones and flashy colors, but it is more interesting to do so with artistry and subtlety in wood or brass or copper.

At one time, the size of the cases was very important to John, as he used them to carry his own cigarettes, and they had to accommodate the brand he smoked then, rather long and filtered. There was a standard size of case for him, and they could be no smaller. Like a magic trick, he would pull one out of his pocket, a brilliant blue or red enamel, or a dark green jade, select a cigarette and light it, and the extraordinary work of art would disappear again into his pocket, like sleight of hand, as the person watching him would stare for long moments after, wondering what they had seen there, or if it had been imagined. It made quite an impression.

Eventually, he gave up smoking, sensibly, and suddenly it became "just a collection," so he became less particular about the size of the boxes he sought and we purchased. It opened up new possibilities for him, and opportunities for me to buy cases in a wider variety of sizes.

There are elements about the boxes that he is more familiar with than I am. The hinges must be perfect and work flawlessly, or the boxes instantly come under suspicion. A true Fabergé case has hinges as smooth as silk, and John has an expert's eye for detecting the slightest imperfection. Similarly, with stones that were added later on, or allegedly imperial insignia. Apparently there are a number of more ordinary cases that were doctored later on, and are not what they pretend to be. John is quick to detect that.

One of my favorite stories in this vein was about a box that was being sold at auction, and had caused great consternation among the cognoscenti. There were whispered suspicions, darkly muttered remarks. At first, it was thought to be a fake, and then it was declared to be authentic. Wanting to surprise him with something truly remarkable—it was an unusual, highly decorated, and very valuable box—I secretly signed up to bid for it at auction. And the bidding was lively, and expensive. Gasping at my own foolishness, I went way, way, way out on a limb, and allowed myself to bid far beyond what I should have, but I felt certain this would be a real showstopper in his collection. I stopped, finally, dizzy, only to be outbid by someone even crazier than I was. And with a mixture of regret and relief, I bowed out as the underbidder.

The next morning, at breakfast, John and I were chatting over the paper, when he mentioned with a guffaw that some poor fool had bought a possible fake Fabergé case the day before at an astronomical price at auction. Apparently, unbeknownst to me, all the experts had conferred again and reversed their most recent decision. It had been decided that, in their opinion, the piece was exquisite, but most likely not made by Fabergé. And John was highly amused that someone had been stupid enough to buy it at the price it went for. Gulp. I sat there, quietly choking on my Wheaties. I had almost been that fool, and but for the grace of God. I looked up rather sheepishly, and confessed that I had been the underbidder. He looked horrified, and I thanked my lucky stars that I had gone no further. That would have been a rather major "oops" in the history of my collecting for him. Very oops indeed. So much for that one.

So, as you can see, this collecting business is heady stuff. Expensive, exciting, addictive, rather like gambling, in its own way. Even now, I look at photographs and auction catalogues, and flirt with the idea of buying a case, though the impetus for my collecting has dwindled. And by now the prices have outrun me. But they still hold a certain fascination. There is a magic to them.

Living with a collector makes "uncluttered" unimaginable, and dusting a nightmare. But somehow, there is always room for one more. There is always one that is just a tiny fraction of a hair different. There is always a reason to buy just one more. There is always another dealer, another shop, another name, another source, another auction . . . and just one more case to add to the collection. It is a kind of madness. A friendly madness, a warm one. And no one's eyes light up like those of a collector in pursuit of such an

Interior detail of case shown on p. 50 with the inscription "To dear Nicky from Mama, 6th May, 1900."

object. . . . Ha! Gotcha! It is the way some men feel about women, and others about stuffed alligators, or birds, or gold boxes. To each his passion.

As for John Traina, his collection is beyond remarkable. It is unique in the world. It bears the stamp of his impeccable taste and style, combined with the art of Carl Fabergé and the delicate hand of his workmasters. It is an unfailing combination. Few men, if any, have the style or eye of John Traina, or the collection he does.

And as for me, having given up both the collection and the collector, they no longer hold quite the same magic for me. But even now, or fifty years from now, I will still have a tear in my eye when I read the inscription "To Nicky, love, Mama" and think what it meant to her when she bought it for him, and him when he received it. It will always make me think of my Nicky. And I will always dream of being so loved by a man that he would wish to be alive only on my lips . . . and extinguished the moment he left them. In my heart, if not theirs, those lovers will live forever.

It is a noble passion, collecting. It provides beauty for the rest of us to look at, but I do not have the time, or the energy, or the inclination to seek out these beauties. I growl when there are more than two things on my coffee table, and I am happier if the things on it were made by my children. John has given countless people pleasure by lending many of the cases to museums for people to view, and people tell me constantly how much they enjoyed them. The world needs its John Trainas. And having growled, and having fussed, and having shuffled the cases around and complained about their expense and their use- lessness, and having fought over them at times, I nonetheless admire the collection. And with a warm heart, and my love, I still say, "Long Live the Collector!"

Fabergé's Russia

THE HISTORY of the Fabergé cigarette case ("as Russian as Tchaikovsky," said H. C. Bainbridge) and the Fabergé firm is closely linked to St. Petersburg.

St. Petersburg, founded by Peter the Great in 1703 as his "window to the West," brought the Russian giant closer to Europe's shores and the Continent closer to Russia. The Russia of the Czars was four-fifths in Asia and one-fifth in Europe, so St. Petersburg was truly where East and West met, a sort of doorstep to Europe. St. Petersburg was a magnificent European-style city of grand palaces, gardens, and colorful buildings built on both banks of the Neva River and the islands in its delta. The architecture was not at all Russian but instead reflected the styles Peter had seen in Amsterdam, London, and Venice. This influence lent an international flavor to the grand city, which was declared the official Russian capital in 1712.

This home of Fabergé, once called the "Venice of the North" (in reference to the many waterways crisscrossing the city), also held a less vaulted nickname, described by Steve Raymer in *St. Petersburg:*

> St. Petersburg owes its existence to forced labor and coercion. From across his empire, Czar Peter summoned carpenters, stonecutters, masons and laborers to build his capital. They lived in crowded and filthy huts, toiled in swamps and bogs, and died in droves from malaria, scurvy, and dysentery. In Peter's day somewhere between 40,000 and 100,000 Russian peasants and Swedish prisoners-of-war perished while building St. Petersburg. Petersburgers would speak for generations of "psychic energy" radiating from the corpses that, literally, made up the city's early foundation. To this day, Russians call St. Petersburg "a city built on bones."

However, Peter the Great's vision of his new capital was that of an imposing city built of stone. Since there was no stone naturally occurring in the hostile swampy territory, he required all the ships and wagons entering the city to bring in a certain number of stones. Eventually, Russian wooden architecture (which he had painted to look like masonry) dominated his city, which became known for its educational, technological, military, political, and cultural achievements, all of which are still enjoyed by Petersburgers today.

In 1914, Czar Nicholas II felt that the city should have a Russian name and it was changed to Petrograd; then in 1924 the Soviets renamed it Leningrad; and in 1991 it once again became St. Petersburg.

This city of glamour, excitement, and opportunity served as a beacon to artists, merchants, and craftsmen worldwide. Many came to visit, and many stayed and became "Russianized," disseminating their varied cultures and impregnating the city with an international flair and aristocratic character. St. Petersburg became a melting pot of artisans from Germany, France, Italy, Holland, Finland, and Sweden, all of whom lent their own nationalistic flavor to their crafts. The decorative art of Fabergé in many ways corresponded to this "melt." Peter died in 1725, and his bones were eventually moved to St. Petersburg for burial—an act which lent a greater feeling of history to the city.

The reign of the Romanoffs after 1842, when the House of Fabergé was founded in St. Petersburg, was closely related to Fabergé in what has been called a unique "marriage." Czar Alexander III appointed the House of Fabergé by royal warrant as one of the goldsmiths and jewelers to the Court in 1885, so it must be assumed that the firm supplied the Romanoffs before that time and was rewarded with patronage and commissions, including the imperial Easter eggs. These eggs were ordered each year as gifts to the Czarina throughout the reign of Nicholas II (1894 to the revolution of 1917). It should be noted, though, that some cigarette cases at the time were more expensive than imperial eggs.

The Romanoffs (known to be by far the wealthiest of dynasties) had a history of showing their wealth to impress and, in some cases, subject their princes, khans, emirs, and neighbors. In Europe this was recognized, as was their opulence. It was fitting that Fabergé should conduct his craft in this capital of wealth, royalty, and nobility and appeal to the taste of the court, nobles, visitors, and kings and queens of Europe and elsewhere. Even the French, who were leaders of culture and jewelry, recognized that they couldn't do the same things as were done in St. Petersburg.

St. Petersburg, the Imperial City, was the home of Fabergé. The firm's European craftsmen, many of whom were from Finland, worked in St. Petersburg just as Europeans designed and adorned St. Petersburg in the days of Peter the Great. All the imperial Easter eggs were made in St. Petersburg, as were most of the enamel, lapidary, and gold cases. The nearness of Fabergé to his workmen accounted for most of the skilled work from St. Petersburg. On Fabergé's relationship with his workmasters, H. C. Bainbridge wrote in *Peter Carl Fabergé*:

He was always doing something which so captivated the hearts of those working for him that they reacted at once and gave tit for tat, with the result that not only were thousands of beautiful things scattered all the world over but . . . every one of these things possessed the same characteristics, although each of them was largely the product of a separate pair of hands.

With his expanding business and the personnel that went with it, Fabergé knew that he needed larger quarters. With this in mind, he established his home, shop, and factory on St. Petersburg's "Diamond Row," at 24 Bolshaya Morskaya Street. It was the foremost of many extraordinary jewelry houses on the street. Designed in 1898 by Karl Schmidt (Fabergé's nephew), this new venue contained Fabergé's workshops, salesrooms, design studio, apartment, and offices. Purchased for half a million rubles, the four-story double-winged building was completed in 1900 and is still located at the center of the historic district in St. Petersburg. Some of the unique historical features include a distinctive rusticated granite and polished marble facade, a formal entrance staircase surmounted by a series of stained-glass windows, and also an elevator (constructed as a safe) that Carl Fabergé used to take his night's work upstairs.

The workshops of Fabergé workmasters Michael Perchin, Henrik Wigström, Albert Holmström, August Hollming, Alfred Thielemann, Viktor Aarne, Hjalmar Armfelt, Andrei Gorianov, Anders Nevalainen, Feodor Afanassiev, and Vladimir Soloviev were there and were listed as being part of the vital Fabergé establishment at 24 Bolshaya Morskaya.

As of 1998, the Fabergé Arts Foundation, based in Washington, D.C., may undertake the task of restoring 24 Bolshaya Morskaya as a monument to Fabergé's work and transform the building into a museum and center for education. The restored House of Fabergé would be used for exhibitions, workshops for jewelers, a library and documentation center, a café, a gift shop, and administrative offices. In doing so, the foundation hopes to help the city restore Bolshaya Morskaya to its prerevolutionary commercial and cultural prominence.

This St. Petersburg shop drew through its doors probably the most noble and elite clientele that one could imagine. Customers included the kings and queens of England, Denmark, Greece, Bulgaria, Italy, Norway, Portugal, Spain, Sweden, Egypt, and Siam, as well as such other notables and luminaries as the Duchess of Cumberland, the Aga Khan, Princess Irene of Prussia, the Duchess of Marlborough, Princess Victoria of Battenberg, the Grand Duchess Sergei of Russia, the Grand Duchess of Hesse (and all the other Grand Dukes and Grand Duchesses), the Maharaja of Bikanir, Princess Cecile Murat, Grand Duke Michael and Countess Torby, the Princes of Saxony, the Grand Duke of Weimar, Leopold de Rothschild, Lady Diana Cooper, Youssoupoffs, Stroganoffs, Galitzines, Orloffs, Henry Walters, J. P. Morgan, Emmanuel Nobel, the Kelchs, and Mrs. George Keppel. In 1887 Fabergé's Moscow branch was opened, the Odessa branch in 1890, the London branch in 1903, and the Kiev branch in 1905.

The style of many cigarette cases made in Moscow contrasted with that of those from "worldly" St. Petersburg. The Moscow style reflected Russian arts, culture, tradition, and folklore. Moscow, which was inhabited more than five thousand years ago, was founded in 1147 and was formalized by Ivan III in 1485. Moscow's long history was emphasized in the traditions that even Fabergé recognized. While St. Petersburg meant "European," the Moscow cases can be distinguished by slavic tradition, and in the markings by the use of the double-headed eagle (the establishment in St. Petersburg did not find it necessary to use this symbol).

By the early twentieth century, Fabergé was renowned for making the best of enamel and goldsmith art. He was not only the favorite of the Czar and the Court of St. Petersburg, but the world's best-known jeweler.

Cigarette cases were the rage. Cases were among the first gifts thought of for anniversaries, birthdays, ceremonial events, and for official presentation. The Czar even carried a number of them in his luggage when he traveled, both for these presentation gifts, and for his own use; he could use a different one every day. The Czar smoked, as did the imperial family—his teenage children were even encouraged to smoke—and friends. Smoking was a popular pastime in Russia as well as in the West. According to historian Valentin Skurlov, the Czar smoked Saatchi and Mangubi cigarettes, made in Odessa from Turkish and Egyptian tobacco. He also kept supplies of the tobacco and often rolled his own cigarettes.

Most Russian smokers got their tobacco supply from Soviet Georgia and usually smoked long paper cigarette tubes, or "papirosa," which consisted of about two-thirds tube and about one-third tobacco. The cigarettes produced a very distinctive aroma (which some Westerners prefer to that of the smoke produced by Western cigarettes), and were rather primitively made, unfiltered and powerful. One visitor to Russia at the time referred to the "scent of Russia," which was the combination of the smell of a popular cigarette's smoke with the fragrance of a widely used type of soap. It has been said that this unforgettable scent filled the air of Russia. The cigarette brand referred to was Sobranya.

In the Hermitage the imperial Cabinet was said to contain many Fabergé items at the ready for the Czar or his palace officials to choose from at a moment's notice for trips and state occasions. On their travels, Their Imperial Majesties would bring thirty-two big boxes filled with potential gifts. The boxes would contain portraits of the reigning monarchs and all sorts of materials, including cigarette cases and watches and clocks of different sizes. Huge orders were placed in anticipation of these events. Among the items available were cigarette cases in a variety of styles and prices, as well as jewelry such as pins, tie pins, and brooches, some of which were designated for the cultural centers of the city—the ballet, orchestra, and theater.

Eugene Fabergé, one of Carl's sons, would check inventory and restock the imperial Cabinet once a month. Fabergé became the primary supplier to the Cabinet, exceeding such rivals as Bolin, Inanov, and Morozov. The workshop in St. Petersburg kept an equally large stock and sketches for customers to either choose from or adapt to their taste. Fabergé himself kept a sort of "cabinet" room where he would maintain a private stock to show his special customers. When these clients arrived, he could thus produce a secret treasure—giving them an exclusive view of the piece—which would romanticize it further. The "gift" shop provided for the occasional gifts needed—items were expensive but not unusually so. The Fabergé ledgers indicate the cigarette cases between 1912 and 1913, for example, were sold at the following prices: silver: £7 to £20; enamel: £21 to £40; hardstone: £35 to £80; gold: £63 to £120. The fact that Fabergé made use of mail order by publishing a catalogue is another way that he was unique and ahead of his time.

Quoting from an 1899 Fabergé catalogue, Géza von Habsburg notes that Fabergé claimed:

> Taking account of both the needs of the higher classes of society as well as the interests of the middle class, we provide both the luxury and expensive goods to satisfy the most refined taste as well as the unexpensive goods within the reach of the not too well-to-do.

The hundreds—perhaps thousands—of cigarette cases produced were all under the supervision of Fabergé himself, who ensured the high standards of expertise and quality found in all his pieces.

The invention of the cigarette lighter around 1911 changed the design of some of the Fabergé cases, as tinder cords and match compartments were no longer needed, and separate match cases became redundant. Therefore cases could be sleeker and lighter. Fabergé was quick to incorporate new technologies and modern ideas. Indeed, his ability to adapt his art to ongoing technological developments was an important factor in his success. In keeping with the times, he offered frames for precious photographs and helped popularize the electric pushbell, which replaced the handbell at the table to summon servants.

One of the guiding forces for the evolving Fabergé style was the "World of Art" movement, or Mir Iskusstva, which abandoned the heavy nationalistic art of Old Russia in favor of the artistic traditions of eighteenth- and early-nineteenth-century Europe. Mir Iskusstva was founded in 1898 and included writers and artists such as Sergey Diaghilev, Alexandre Benois, Evgeniy Lanceray, Léon Bakst, and Konstantin Somov, who played an important role in helping to intertwine different aspects of the world of art and literature. The movement extended its reach not only to the visual arts—bringing impressionism to painting and modernism to sculpture—but also to the applied arts, such as porcelain. St. Petersburg became the center of this artistic movement, which was recognized internationally.

When World War I started in 1914, one out of every two workers in Russia had taken part in some labor protest and the imperial family was in isolation. The war brought the Czar and his family into the mainstream of the fight for a short time, during which Fabergé's St. Petersburg factory produced war goods. Fabergé made some patriotic and military-use pieces as well as cigarette cases, most commonly in brass and copper; silver was reserved for the officers. The typical cases were simple and with the double-headed eagle crest. For those wanting better pieces, gunmetal cigarette cases were fashioned to the taste of the buyer. Additionally, according to sources at the Hermitage, round, shallow drinking cups were made to fit into a soldier's pocket. These have commonly and mistakenly been referred to as ashtrays, as the resemblance is striking (see p.148). (However, the imperial eagle was never used in such a manner.) As with other items made for soldiers, the higher the rank, the better the metal used for the cups. Presentation pieces included Red Cross items, eggs, and even badges in 1916 with the silver eagle for the Society for Aid to Soldiers, Their Families and Victims of the War.

War, strikes, riots, three million soldiers dead, government collapse, civil wars, and eventually the Soviets's taking charge of Petrograd spelled the end of St. Petersburg as the capital and the end of the reign of the Romanoffs. The Russian Revolution changed everything. The House of Fabergé was closed down in 1918. Carl Fabergé fled to Switzerland and died two years later, a refugee from his beloved Russia. Citizens were exhorted to keep artworks from being ruined or smuggled out of the country. In November 1917 the Executive Committee of Soviets in Petrograd proclaimed: "Citizens! The old rulers of the country are gone. A gigantic inheritance has been left behind which now belongs to the entire people. Citizens! Protect this inheritance." Still, some of the estimated two million refugees who fled to Europe and the West were able to smuggle out many Fabergé objects.

In fact, after the revolution, the Soviets actively preserved art by collecting valuables. One such item recorded was a cigarette case that was discovered on a chair in the Winter Palace in 1917. In it were cigarettes of the brand smoked by Alexandra Feodorovna, an eerie reminder of the life so tragically interrupted and testament to the daily use of Fabergé's items of function.

Many cases and other Fabergé pieces that were taken out of Russia were traded along the way. Even Fabergé himself used his treasures to gain access to borders. As his granddaughter Tatiana Fabergé recounts: At one border crossing, a patrol guard confiscated a Russian wooden nesting doll from Fabergé and gave it to his own daughter. Unbeknownst to the guard, Fabergé had hidden many gems inside to use as money once he had arrived at his destination. Imagine the surprise of the daughter.

Of course, Paris and London were traditional sales outlets but some Fabergé pieces even traveled the Trans Siberian Railroad east from St. Petersburg to Vladivostock—then to Harbin, Shanghai, and other ports in Asia—perhaps even ending in the United States, where the world's greatest inventory is now housed. (At present the St. Petersburg museums have perhaps less than 150 pieces out of the tens of thousands of pieces produced.)

The art—this symbol of Fabergé's Russia—that came from the West to St. Petersburg moved back to the West again. Its movement echoed that of Fabergé's fame, which had spread from St. Petersburg to the outside world.

The Making of Fabergé's Cigarette Cases

N THE FOREWORD to H. C. Bainbridge's *Peter Carl Fabergé* Sacheverell Sitwell wrote:

> Why, and how is it, that so simple an object as a *cigarette case* can speak to us with a Russian accent, and be as strong of flavour as a phrase out of a Russian song? The cigarette case can be in "red" or "green" or "yellow" gold; it does not matter. The finished object, as you handle it, is as "Russian" as any character in Russian history.

Romanoff Czar Alexander III appointed Fabergé jeweler and goldsmith to the Court in 1884; the Fabergé period of Russian history abruptly ends with the Russian Revolution in 1917. In such a short time, how did the influence of Fabergé extend to almost every corner of the world? How did the Fabergé cigarette case influence the turn of the century? Fabergé as art triumphed beyond his image as a great goldsmith. The craftsmanship of the Fabergé factories was recognized then, as it is today. The extraordinary world reach of Fabergé had to be answered then, as now, in several ways and is explained below.

At the turn of the century Europe was fascinated with the vastness of Russia and Russia's great wealth. Fabergé was European yet Russian. His most skilled craftsmen—his workmasters—were Finns, Swedes, Englishmen, Germans, Estonians, and other Balts, and Poles, as well as Russians. His designers were all of the above plus Swiss, Irish, Lettonians, and Italians. His European training, his French ancestry, and his European managers, all molded into a Russian clay, worked together to produce a particular and renowned Russian art form.

The vast size, wealth, and complexity of the Russian Empire allowed for this brand of World/Russian art, as did the variety and origin of the Fabergé customers. British, French, Scandinavians, Americans, khans, Kings, Queens, Emperors, and aristocracy of many and varied countries added to the flavor and mix. The fact that the factories made to order to the extent they did kept the Russian-foreign mix going. Workmasters were allowed to do their imaginative, unique skilled work, and the customers were encouraged to make their custom requests—all under the quality-guiding hand of Carl Fabergé.

The pieces of art were always kept diverse both in subject and influence by the customers, and the techniques, never stagnant or automatic, were versatile with each request so different. But attention was always paid to detail. Fabergé factories were kept "alive" also by the commercial training of Carl Fabergé. Whether his clients were imperial or royal patrons or ordinary customers, they were all expertly handled by Fabergé. He managed his workmasters with equal skill.

In the early 1900s, the House of Fabergé was indeed a busy place, with orders pouring in from around the world. Over 150,000 items were sold. Three hundred craftsmen in St. Petersburg and two hundred in Moscow were not enough to keep up with the demand. Outside craftsmen had to be commissioned. Carl Fabergé's three sons, Eugene, Agathon, and Alexander, joined the firm, acting as designers along with Franz Birbaum, who had a strong influence on the ultimate designs of the pieces produced by the Fabergé firm. Most of the cigarette cases were manufactured at the St. Petersburg factory and head establishment, but others were made at the Odessa, Kiev, London, and Moscow branches. Styles of the cases often reflected their origin: those with a European flavor were from St. Petersburg; Russian styles were from Moscow; and the more worldly pieces came from London.

Russia's size and extensive natural resources led to the use of a variety of materials to suit the taste of the individual cigarette-case customers. Russia mined stones like lapis lazuli, rhodonite, quartz, citrine, nephrite jade, pink jade, jasper, gray jasper, malachite, labradorite, bowenite, fluorite, kalgan, olivine, amazonite, Siberian amethyst, turquoise, rock crystal, moss agate, chalcedony, agate, aventurine quartz, obsidian, and carnelian. Some of the minerals came from Russia's borders in the Himalayas.

Mines in the Urals, Siberia, and Caucasus were providers of such gems as diamonds, rubies, Siberian emeralds, sapphires, moonstones, chrysoberyls, topaz, and garnets. These were used by Fabergé lapidaries for thumbpieces and decoration. Russia also mined great quantities of gold and silver, which were used by Fabergé. Nephrite, particularly the "spinach jade" color, was often withheld from sale to the public, as it was so popular with the Czar. It was mined for the most part in the Irkutsk mountains near Lake Baikal and also near Altai, not in the Urals.

If stones and minerals wouldn't do, cases were made of Russian woods—holly, Karelian birch, oak, walnut, or palisander from the Crimea—or glass, crystal, tortoiseshell, shagreen, and leather. These materials were not ordinarily used by goldsmiths, and their use made clear something very different about Fabergé—he was less concerned about the value of his pieces derived from the price of their raw materials than he was with the value they derived from their overall beauty and workmanship.

Fabergé craftsmen used combinations of metal and stone to produce purpurine, which was invented by a craftsman named Petouchoff of the Imperial Glass Factory in St. Petersburg. This rare substance had a rich red color and a heaviness deriving from the gold in its composition. Purpurine has never been re-created since the death of its creator. It is perhaps the rarest natural or artificial substance employed by Fabergé. He also favored the Mecca stone, found on the Arabian peninsula, and he typically used a type with a light-blue color, though the stones also occur in pinkish tones and can be artificially tinted.

The colors of gold Fabergé used were outstanding and provided great variety to the goldsmith. Not only did he make full use of colors of gold but also of their finish.

Examples of plain polished gold as well as matte gold and gold samorodok—which has a nugget-like finish (see p. 101)—can be seen in this collection. Fabergé's workmasters perfected two methods of creating golds of different shades and intensities. The first method was to mix alloys. Pure gold is 24 carats, but is too soft for items as large as Fabergé's cases, so it has to be mixed with harder metals; the metals mixed in with the gold alter its resulting color. Fabergé used precise portions of copper (to achieve a red gold), silver (to achieve a green gold), and nickel and palladium in various combinations to come up with gold alloys (usually 14 carats) varying from green to red, yellow, blue, orange, and gray.

The second method, which Fabergé used less frequently, was simply to tint the finished pieces. The *quatre couleur* technique employed in the Fabergé workshops allowed the workmasters to use four colors of gold within the same piece; often the hues are enhanced by the addition of stones and/or enamels. The colors are subtle but can be cleverly applied to bows, swags, and leaf borders. A wonderful example of this technique is seen on page 69.

Fabergé cases were personal objects. They were made to be carried around, not to be admired in a vitrine. They had to *feel* good. They had to fit a pocket or purse, have smooth corners and surfaces. The stones, the clasps, the hinges, the decorations, the crests, the initials had to have the carrier's comfort and carrier's touch in mind. In fact, after holding one of Fabergé's cigarette cases for a moment, Queen Alexandra said "There is one thing about all Fabergé pieces; they are so satisfying." Fabergé cases can still be recognized by their touch.

All these minerals, substances, mechanical attachments, and decorations needed to be molded into a "practical" or "functional" art form to be carried around the globe. These cases were attractive without being bulky or uncomfortable. Gentlemen all over Europe saw the need for a Fabergé case in 1900, and those finished in ribbed gold were the most popular.

The Fabergé workmen could use the flat surface provided by a cigarette case as a canvas for their art. Fabergé's mission was to bring this flatness alive through the use of wood, metal, stone, and above all enamel, which could be worked to its best advantage on the flat surface of a case. The enamels of Fabergé became a trademark of the time, even recognized by other firms as Fabergé's preserve. They are still recognized as such; they are still unequaled.

The basic methods Fabergé used with enamel were not new, most having been popularized in late-eighteenth-century Europe. But the methods had fallen out of use, and it was Fabergé who revived and perfected them. By 1900 Fabergé was producing the world's finest works of enamel. His precise method remained a guarded secret, but the general principles are known. He applied multiple layers of enamel—typically five or six—over a metallic base of silver or 14 carat gold. The metal base would first be engraved with lines and dots, often giving it a sort of geometric or wave pattern which would remain visible through the enamel. There were many variations of *guilloché*, or engine turning, which produced a variety of effects, giving the pieces a feeling of texture and depth (while remaining smooth) and allowing them to have a sunburst, wave, or moiré background.

The cigarette cases were fabricated first and then enameled. The work was done without warping or shrinking, a challenge still encountered today. The enamels were fired at the extremely high temperatures of 700 to 800 degrees Celsius. Sometimes effects such as painted objects or scenes would be applied to the next-to-last layer of enamel. Finally there were hours of painstaking buffing and polishing on a wheel to gloss the enamel's surface.

Fabergé continually researched new colors for cigarette case enamels, often naming them as the customer wished. Their translucent surfaces still glow in these "over the rainbow" varieties. It was said that accidents often resulted in the creation of some unusual color that could not later be duplicated. In fact, even the enamelers themselves considered every piece to be enameled a new experiment. The rareness of good-condition enamel cases today is due to later accidents and the fragility of glass enamel. But Fabergé colors are well recognized; there were said to be at least 150 shades. For example, there were twenty-five blues in Fabergé's palette; Cartier, by contrast, had only sixty color shades in total. While surely one of the most magnificent colors he offered was oyster, which, when turned in the hand produced the wonderful shimmering, changing reflections of a seashell, he also provided raspberry and strawberry reds, lime green, lovebird green, emerald green, royal blue, cobalt blue, sky blue, sea blue, periwinkle blue, evening blue, aquamarine, turquoise, rust, primrose yellow, golden yellow, salmon pink, plum mauve, lavender, battleship gray, and opalescent pink, to name a few. Many times ladies would request a special color be made to match a particular gown or handbag, which allowed further experimentation and creativity by the Fabergé workers. Pink was the Czarina's favorite color.

Just the right colored stones or gemstones were searched for to finish combinations of color and textures for the thumbpieces and decorations on the cases. The quality of diamonds, sapphires, or rubies, for example, was not as important as the color tone or compatibility with the rest of the case. Often gems of poorer quality were selected to avoid flashiness. For example, off-color diamonds, considered inferior in their day (but most valuable now) were used to blend properly with the other colors in a case. Again, Fabergé was not known for making a point of utilizing showy, flashy, and costly material. He was more concerned with the visual appeal and substance of the case than its cost. He is quoted in *Fabergé: Imperial Jeweller* as saying, "If we were to compare my business to such firms as Tiffany, Boucheron or Cartier, . . . they are people of commerce rather than artist jewellers. I have little interest in an expensive object if its price is only in the abundance of diamonds and pearls." Better stones might then be used in applying imperial crests or gem-encrusted monograms to relay the message. The varieties, patterns, and textures existed in endless combinations, but the one constant was the quality of the excellent goldsmith.

Many figures have been used over the years to describe the combined number of Fabergé workers, sometimes reported as high as seven hundred. But, thanks to research conducted with records and vaults that have only recently become available, it appears that there were twenty-two workmasters (plus several additional but unidentified signatures associated with the Fabergé marks) and over five hundred—perhaps even six hundred—employees in the factories and shops, making the firm the largest of its type at the time. The amazing thing about his employees was that they all seemed to work of the same mind. The result was perfection.

Mother Russia borrowed from the art of Egypt, Rome, Siam, Greece, Japan, China, Italian Renaissance, and French Louis for case motifs. Much was taken from ancient art, from nature, and from modern styles but always with a Russian Fabergé master hand guiding it. The Slavic motifs, many from the Moscow factory, were traditionally gold, and the customary cloisonné painted enamel was provided for Russian taste. Nationalistic Russia and World War I affected the styles and tastes. Contemporary jewelry designer Christopher English Walling comments that Fabergé did his own "cleaner" version of the "barbaric" Russian style, as well as Baroque and Rococo styles when he needed to, resulting in an elegant simplicity. The nationalistic case styles continued beyond Fabergé and the revolution into the Soviet period. Some examples are shown on page 152.

Up until then the Fabergé workmasters, factories, lapidaries, designers, and salesmen took pride in using the jewelers' art to create such useful pieces as cigarette cases, bell pushes, cane handles, picture frames, inkwells, pen holders, paper knives, stamp holders, powder compacts, table lighters, cigar cutters, soldier's drinking cups, scent bottles, tea and coffee services, and clocks rather than jewelry and other items of adornment.

But the cases expressed the most. The cases tell the whole Fabergé story.

The Cases in the
Collection

O F ALL the productions of Fabergé, even counting the Imperial Easter Eggs, flowers, animals and all the other objects of fantasy, and if the lapse of time is finally to give Fabergé a place which can never be assailed, the same which the comparatively few who know him give to him now and that on a par with the makers of the Eighteenth Century French snuff boxes (and do not let us forget the English), I say of all the productions of Fabergé, it is, in my opinion, his cigarette cases which should finally bring about this happy consummation.

—H. C. Bainbridge, *Peter Carl Fabergé*

The cases presented in this book (from a collection accumulated over twenty years) are a study of the broad variety of skills, art, colors, and materials used by Fabergé and his workmasters.

They are expertly photographed by Fred Lyon (whose photographic career has included gems, fashion, wine, food, art, and places akin to the history and art of the cases that follow), whose work allows a reader to enjoy both the *visual* and *functional* appeal of the cases. Some interesting interiors, inscriptions, outer presentation boxes, and art details have also been offered to give one a closer taste of the esthetic pleasures of Fabergé.

Research into the inventory marks, workmaster's marks, hallmarks, export marks, gold and silver standards, crowns, crests, initials, and monograms continues. This process, conducted with Elizabeth Roman, a gem and jewelry expert, was one of the most interesting parts of creating this book. The signs are there to be searched in each case, and sometimes the lack of signs can tell a story too. The bumps, scratches, and dents are witness to the use and personality of the cases. These interior and exterior markings have added to the delight of opening each case and impart a sort of persona to each one. Photographer Fred Lyon has captured these personalities.

With this wide range of photographed cases, one can more easily compare and see the differences in workmasters, designers, materials, and styles of the time. One can also identify the various workshops and factories used by Fabergé versus his competitors, such as Hahn, Britzin, and other factories producing presentation pieces for the imperial Court. Even the Bolsheviks and Communists duplicated the Fabergé and Slavic styles. The photographs will allow the reader to recognize the styles of imperial and historical Russia, as well as those borrowed and incorporated into the Fabergé style.

In order to help the reader appreciate some details of the individual cases represented in this book, I have included in each caption the following information:

- hallmarks, when visible
- Russian state hallmarks (indicating city and date)
- length
- inventory numbers, if visible
- any known provenance

In many cases, the Fabergé name appears in different forms on those pieces without the hallmark of an individual workmaster. Others bear only initials—indicating that there was only a small area for the punch—or other marks signifying that the articles were being exported to the European market. It should be noted that not all Fabergé objects bear the marks of the House or the workmasters. Fabergé awarded his St. Petersburg workers the privilege of having their initials on their finished pieces—a privilege not generally extended to workers in Moscow. This helps explain the lack of marks on many pieces.

The Russian state hallmarks and symbols are well documented in other books on Fabergé. I have included the information for city and period in which the piece was made. Additionally, workmasters are acknowledged by name or initials in the captions, some of whom are "known unknowns" usually associated with the Fabergé marks.

I hope that you will enjoy the collection that I enjoy.

opposite:
Silver-gilt case decorated with gray-green *guilloché* enamel in sunburst pattern. The lid is further ornamented with a four-leaf clover with rose-cut diamonds on stem and leaves. Interior with engraved Russian inscription in the hand of Empress Marie Feodorovna: "To dear Nicky from Mama, 6th May, 1900" (see p. 36).
Initials of AUGUST HOLLMING, FABERGÉ in Cyrillic.
St. Petersburg 1896–1908. 3⅞"

Presented by Empress Marie Feodorovna to her son Czar Nicholas II on his thirty-second birthday. The gray-green is the color of the Preobrajensky Regiment, to which he belonged. This regiment, which was founded by Peter the Great, was the most prestigious.

above, clockwise from left:
Silver-gilt case enameled battleship gray over moiré *guilloché* ground. Cabochon sapphire thumbpiece. The lid is engraved "1946 November 29."
St. Petersburg 1908–17. 3⅞"

Silver-gilt case enameled battleship gray over waved *guilloché* ground with gold-mounted cabochon sapphire thumbpiece.
Initials of JAKOV ROSEN. St. Petersburg 1908–17. 3⅞"

Silver-gilt case with light-gray translucent enamel over waved *guilloché* ground. Etched gold rim and ruby thumbpiece.
Initials of HENRIK WIGSTRÖM. St. Petersburg 1896–1908. 3⅞"

opposite:
Enamel, nephrite, and rhodonite silver-gilt
case of white translucent enamel over waved
geometric pattern with a rectangular panel of
nephrite and rhodonite bands. Cabochon ruby
thumbpiece set in gold.
Initials of ANDRE KARLOVICH ADLER. St. Petersburg 1908–17.
3¾″
Is said to have once been owned by a Grand Duke.

above:
A three-color gold case with chased scalework.
Cabochon sapphire thumbpiece.
Initials of OSKAR PIHL, KFABERGÉ in Cyrillic.
Moscow pre-1896. 3⅜″. Exhibitions: "Fabergé and Finland";
"Fabergé: Loistavaa Kultasepäntaidetta"
*One of the few known pieces by Pihl, father of
Fabergé designer Alma Pihl.*

clockwise from top right:

Gold shagreen-like case with gold thumbpiece. Engraved inside with French inscription *"Capitaine F. Chevalier En Souvenir des services rendus a la Flotte Volontaire Russe"* ("Captain F. Chevalier In remembrance of services made to the Russian Volunteer Fleet").
Initials of NICHOLS and PLINCKE. St. Petersburg pre-1896. 3⅜"

A two-color gold cigarette case. Its entire body is decorated with alternating red and green gold bands, further ornamented with crisscrossing lines forming diamond shapes. Cabochon sapphire thumbpiece.
KHLEBNIKOV, imperial warrant. Moscow 1908–17. 4⅛"

A gold rectangular case. Its entire body is chased and repoussé with stylized cacao fruit, with hinged match compartment and striker plate. Cabochon emerald thumbpiece.
FABERGÉ in Cyrillic. St. Petersburg 1896–1908. 3⅜"

A polished gold case with wavy pattern. Cabochon sapphire thumbpiece.
Initials of GABRIEL NIUKKANEN. St. Petersburg 1908–17. 3⅜"

Hammered-gold case of oval section, with match compartment and cabochon sapphire thumbpiece. Interior inscribed "Gross Papa Mickey, 9 April 1901."
Initials of AUGUST HOLLMING, FABERGÉ in Cyrillic. St. Petersburg 1896–1908. 3⅜"

A two-color gold polished case engraved with three intertwined braids. Cabochon sapphire thumbpiece.
FEDOR LORIE. Moscow 1908–17. 3⅜"

center:
Russian gold case with sunburst design emanating from the cabochon sapphire set in gold thumbpiece.
3¾"

clockwise from top left:
A silver-gilt and light blue *guilloché* enamel case with sunburst design and cabochon ruby thumbpiece.
Initials of MICHAEL PERCHIN. St. Petersburg 1896–1908. 3½".
Inventory No. 7858

A silver-gilt case decorated with light-blue *guilloché* enamel, fitted with a tassel and a match compartment. Gold thumbpiece is set with a cabochon moonstone.
Initials of ANDRE KARLOVICH ADLER. St. Petersburg 1908–17. 3⅜"

A silver-gilt case. Its entire body is decorated with oyster white moiré *guilloché* enamel. Thumbpiece is set with a row of rose-cut diamonds.
Initials of AUGUST HOLLMING, KFABERGÉ in Cyrillic. St. Petersburg 1908–17. 3⅜". Inventory No. 25433. Exhibition: "Fabergé and Finland"

Silver-gilt and gold-mounted case with light blue translucent enamel over moiré *guilloché* ground, with gold borders chased with acanthus leaves. Striker plate on side of case. Gold-mounted ruby thumbpiece.
Initials of JULIUS RAPPOPORT. St. Petersburg 1908–17. 4".
Exhibition: "Great Fabergé in the Hermitage"
This color blue is reminiscent of interior colors in the Winter Palace.

opposite:

A silver-gilt case with opalescent oyster *guilloché* enamel with sunburst pattern centered on either side of the case. The lid is set with the gold-crowned initials of Grand Duke Nicholas Nicholaevich. Gold oblong thumbpiece.

Initials of AUGUST HOLLMING, FABERGÉ in Cyrillic. St. Petersburg 1908–17. 3⅜″. Exhibition: "Great Fabergé in the Hermitage"

Grand Duke Nicholas Nicholaevich was a cousin of Nicholas II and commanded the Russian forces during 1914 and 1915.

above:

Silver-gilt and steel gray–blue enamel case with sunburst design. The lid is decorated with a crown of Monomakh encrusted with a row of rose-cut diamonds and three stones: ruby, sapphire, and diamond. Thumbpiece is set with a rose-cut diamond.

Initials of AUGUST HOLLMING. St. Petersburg 1908–17. 3⅜″. Inventory No. 1667281. Exhibition: "Fabergé in America"

The crown of Monomakh, which decorates the cover, is a representation of the Byzantine-style Muscovite crown used before the eighteenth century. The original Monomakh crown was used at the coronation of the first Romanoff Czar.

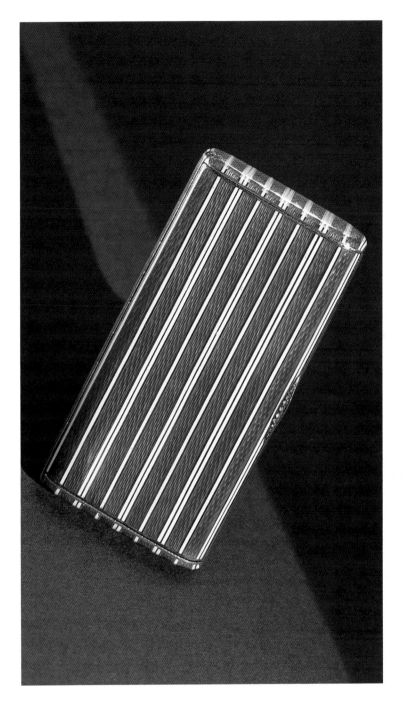

A silver reeded case with imperial warrant. The case is designed with a secret compartment that contains an oval opening for a photograph. Cabochon sapphire thumbpiece.
Initials of ANDERS NEVALAINEN, KFABERGÉ in Cyrillic, imperial warrant. St. Petersburg 1896–1908. 3½″.
Exhibition: "Fabergé and Finland"

above, left:
A gold case decorated with opaque stripes of white enamel, both ends terminating with rounded chalcedony. One end opens as a match compartment. Centered on the lid is the crowned monogram of Prince Alexander. Fitted case. Thumbpiece set with rose-cut diamonds. The interior is inscribed "Victoria Eugenia."
Initials of HENRIK WIGSTRÖM, FABERGÉ. St. Petersburg 1908–17. 3⅜″. Inventory No. 80-321

Prince Alexander Albert of Battenberg (1886–1960), later the Marquess of Carisbrooke, presented the case to Queen Victoria's granddaughter (Victoria Eugenia), the future Queen of Spain. The commission of the box can be seen in the archives of the design

book of Henrik Wigström. The original pencil-and-watercolor design shows the five-digit production number and its completion date, 24 November 1911.

above, right:
Small silver-gilt case. Its body decorated with lavender *guilloché* enamel stripes and thin white opaque enamel stripes. Rose-cut diamond thumbpiece.
Initials of HENRIK WIGSTRÖM, FABERGÉ in Cyrillic. St. Petersburg 1908–17. 3⅜″

above:
The entire body of this gold, enamel, and diamond imperial presentation case is decorated with sunburst *guilloché* ground and translucent red enamel. The lid is applied with a diamond imperial crown. Original fitted case with gilt imperial eagle on the cover. Diamond thumbpiece.
Initials of AUGUST HOLMSTRÖM, FABERGÉ. St. Petersburg, 1896–1908. 3⅝″. Inventory No. 1158. Exhibition: "Fabergé in America"
Presented by Czar Nicholas II to Pavel Kaczkovsky on the eve of the coronation, May 25, 1896, as a token of gratitude for his work as a high-ranking civil servant, thence by descent. The crown depicted is the Grand Imperial crown created for Catherine the Great by Jeremy Posier in the eighteenth century and used at all subsequent coronations. The actual crown weighs five pounds.

opposite:
Silver-gilt imperial presentation case enameled overall in strawberry red over *guilloché* sunburst ground emanating from the crown of Monomakh set with one ruby, one sapphire, and rose-cut diamonds. Gold mounted rose-cut diamond thumbpiece. In original fitted imperial presentation case.
Initials of AUGUST HOLLMING. St. Petersburg 1908–17. 3⅝″. Inventory No. 4188_. Exhibition: "Fabergé in America"
Presented by Nicholas II to the Head of Forests of Poland to commemorate the Romanoff Tercentary.

Silver-gilt case with salmon-pink *guilloché* enamel over sunburst pattern. The cover is applied with a gold imperial eagle
set with a rose-cut diamond. Thumbpiece is also set with a diamond. Original fitted case stamped with imperial warrant,
St. Petersburg, Moscow.

Initials of AUGUST HOLLMING. St. Petersburg 1896–1908. 3⅞″. Inventory No. 4984. Exhibition: "Fabergé in America"

*Presented by the imperial Cabinet on behalf of Czar Nicholas II to Eduard Vella in May 1902 for services rendered at the Russian
consulate in Malta.*

White enamel sunburst pattern emanating from a faceted ruby on the cover of this cigarette and match case set. The cigarette case contains four original cigarettes, and the matchbox contains five original matches and a striker plate on the end. The cigarette case has a ruby thumbpiece, while the one on the matchbox is a row of diamonds.

Initials of AUGUST HOLMSTRÖM, FABERGÉ in Cyrillic. St. Petersburg 1896–1908. Cigarette case: 2⅜″. Matchbox: 1½″.
Case Inventory No.: 4/R/2 529, Box 529 2/. Exhibition: "Carl Fabergé: Goldsmith to the Tsar"

clockwise from top:
Jeweled gunmetal case of curved rectangular form with rounded corners. Set in the front with a crowned rose-diamond monogram "JS" and with gold-mounted sapphire thumbpiece.
3¾″

Jeweled gunmetal vesta case of curved rectangular form with rounded corners. Set in the front with a crowned rose-diamond monogram "JS" and with gold-mounted sapphire thumbpiece.
1¾″

A Russian gunmetal case with a gold monogram and blue cabochon thumbpiece.
3¾″

Gunmetal cigarette case, rectangular, slightly curved, applied with a gold monogram "MT." Thumbpiece set with a faceted red stone. Date is circa 1914–16.
3¾″
The crown over the monogram is not Russian, but European.

clockwise from top:
A gunmetal case with numerous gold monograms and
other applied gold mementos. Cabochon sapphire
thumbpiece.
3½″

Gold-mounted gunmetal case, of rectangular section and
rounded corners. The body hammered overall, with gold
hinge and gold-mounted cabochon sapphire thumbpiece.
3½″

A gunmetal case with two diamond-set opals forming two
side-by-side hearts and a gold-crowned monogram.
Cabochon sapphire thumbpiece.
3⅝″

Gunmetal case applied with a diamond jeweled serpent
and entwined letters "AK." Cabochon sapphire thumbpiece.
3⅝″

65

opposite, clockwise from top left:

A gold and gem-set box, the rectangular hammered body applied with gold stems and leaves with stylized buds and set with cabochon rubies, an emerald, brilliant and rose-cut diamonds, and sapphires. Cabochon sapphire thumbpiece.
Initials of August Holmström. St. Petersburg pre-1896. 3⅜″. Inventory No. 605L

A silver case with a match compartment and a yellow/purple tassel that has a fluted pendant. Its lid is decorated with a single branch and fourteen cabochon rubies. Gilt interior, and inscribed "18 February 1903—Charlotte."
Initials of Michael Perchin, Fabergé in Cyrillic. St. Petersburg 1896–1908. 3¹³⁄₁₆″. Inventory No. 7440

A silver case, the lid decorated with palm fronds and blossoms with cabochon rubies. The stems of the branches are ornamented with rose-cut diamonds. Cabochon sapphire thumbpiece.
KFabergé in Cyrillic with imperial warrant. Moscow 1896–1908. 3⅜″. Inventory No. 11429 and 13490

above, right:

A gold-mounted gunmetal case with match compartment and striker plate, blue tinder cord, and cabochon sapphire thumbpiece.
Initials of Henrik Wigström, Fabergé in Cyrillic. 3½″. Exhibition: "Fabergé"

right, top:

Two-colored gold case with match compartment and wick, of rectangular shape with *guilloché* ground within foliate borders. Both sides set with rose-cut diamond-set signatures; one of Elizaveta with dates 1886 and 1904.
Initials of Henrik Wigström, Fabergé in Cyrillic. St. Petersburg 1896–1908. 3½″. Exhibition: "Fabergé in America"
Said to have been presented by Elizaveta Feodorovna (Elisabeth, princess of Hessen-Darmstadt), wife of Grand Duke Sergei Aleksandrovich and sister of Czarina Alexandra Feodorovna, to her husband, uncle of Czar Nicholas II. Grand Duchess Elizaveta founded the Martha-Mary Convent in Moscow after the assassination of her husband by revolutionaries in 1905. She was killed by the Bolsheviks in 1918 and canonized by the Russian Orthodox Church in 1994.

right, bottom:

A large gold engine-turned case with rounded fluted ends, further decorated with a polished circular reserve in the middle. Cabochon sapphire thumbpiece. Original fitted case.
Initials of Henrik Wigström, Fabergé in Cyrillic. St. Petersburg 1908–17. 5″

Blue *guilloché* enamel over swag design, gold and silver vermeil lady's compact/cigarette case set with a gold fleur-de-lis on the lid.
Initials of Henrik Wigström, Fabergé in Cyrillic. St. Petersburg 1908–17. 4″

Four-color (a *quatre-couleur*) gold box with diamond thumbpiece.
Initials of August Holmström, Fabergé in Cyrillic. St. Petersburg pre-1896. 3½″. Inventory No. 2140

opposite, clockwise from top left:
Silver case with sunburst design emanating from the cabochon sapphire set in gold thumbpiece. Gilt interior.
Initials of PHILIPP THEODOR RINGE. St. Petersburg 1908–17. 4⅛"

Ribbed silver case with five hinged compartments, the gold thumbpiece set with a cabochon sapphire.
KFABERGÉ in Cyrillic, imperial warrant. Moscow 1908–17. 4⅛". Inventory No. 17025
The case was purchased on December 29, 1913, by Grand Duke Michael Alexandrovich (younger brother of Czar Nicholas II) at Fabergé's London branch for £7 (44 rubles). He was killed by the Bolsheviks in 1918.

A silver reeded case with gold-mounted cabochon sapphire thumbpiece. Original fitted case stamped with imperial warrant—St. Petersburg, Moscow, Odessa.
KFABERGÉ in Cyrillic, imperial warrant. Moscow 1908–17. 3⅝". Inventory No. 31458. Exhibition: "Fabergé in America"

Large silver case with horizontal and diagonal reeding, with match compartment and striker plate. Cabochon sapphire thumbpiece.
Initials of AUGUST HOLLMING, FABERGÉ in Cyrillic. English import marks for 1912. St. Petersburg 1908–17. 5⅛". Inventory No. 21278

center:
Silver reeded case with gold-set cabochon sapphire thumbpiece.
Initials of M.C. St. Petersburg 1908–17. 3⅞"

above, top:
A silver reeded case set with a gold 7.5-ruble coin. The obverse shows a profile of Nicholas II, reversed with a Russian imperial crest. The case comes with a fitted silver-trimmed leather case.
Initials of ANDERS NEVALAINEN, KFABERGÉ in Cyrillic. St. Petersburg 1896–1908. 4". Inventory No. 11222

above, bottom:
A silver reeded case. Its lid is set in the center with an eagle with extended wings perched on an enameled Russian imperial flag. The case has a match compartment and striker plate. Gold thumbpiece.
Initials of AUGUST HOLLMING, FABERGÉ in Cyrillic. St. Petersburg 1896–1908. 3⅞". Inventory No. 8417
The most interesting and unusual part about this piece is the secret sliding panel attached to the interior of the lid. The panel has a frame that is designed to hold a rectangular photograph.

opposite:
Two-color gold case, its entire body enameled deep purple over *guilloché* enamel ground, further decorated with two-color gold swags and opaque white enamel trellis. Rose-cut diamond thumbpiece.
KFABERGÉ in Cyrillic, imperial warrant. Moscow pre-1896. 3¼″. Exhibition: "Fabergé in America"

above, clockwise from top left:
Shagreen case mounted with two-color gold. Compressed oval outline decorated with red and green gold rococo scrolls. Diamond thumbpiece.
Initials of MICHAEL PERCHIN, FABERGÉ in Cyrillic. St. Petersburg pre-1896. 3½″. Inventory No. 45037

Unusual openwork silver case with leather lining. The entire body of the case is decorated with scrolling foliage with an anchor in the corner. Cabochon sapphire thumbpiece set in red gold.
ALEXANDER TILLANDER. St. Petersburg pre-1896. 3¼″. Inventory No. 17566

A gold-mounted leather case applied with rococo foliate scrolls and flowers. Gilt interior.
Initials of MICHAEL PERCHIN. St. Petersburg pre-1896. 3½″. Inventory No. 45377

opposite, above:
Case of gold and rhodonite panels bordered with green enamel laurel leaves. The sides are enameled with pink *guilloché* enamel and painted with floral ornament. Rose-cut diamond thumbpiece.
Initials of HENRIK WIGSTRÖM. St. Petersburg 1908–17. 3⅝″

opposite, below:
Tubular case enameled in mauve and mounted in two-color gold. Either end decorated with gold-leaf trim. Thumbpiece decorated with rose-cut diamonds.
Initials of AUGUST HOLLMING, FABERGÉ. St. Petersburg 1896–1908. 3⁷⁄₁₆″. Exhibitions: "Fabergé in America"; "Carl Fabergé: Goldsmith to the Tsar"

above:
Silver-gilt and powder-blue enamel tubular case over moiré *guilloché* ground with match compartment that opens at the end. London hallmarks for the year 1911. Rose-cut diamond thumbpiece.
Initials of AUGUST HOLLMING, CF, London marks. St. Petersburg 1908–17. 3½″. Inventory No. 22617.
Sold on 12/23/1912 to Mrs. Ronald Grenville for £26.

opposite:
Gold and silver-gilt red *guilloché* enamel case decorated
with interlaced diamond-studded initials "CV." Diamond
thumbpiece.
Initials of Henrik Wigström, Fabergé in Cyrillic. St. Petersburg
1896–1908. 3⅞". Exhibition: "Fabergé in America"
*This case belonged to Cornelius Vanderbilt III. His wife was one
of Fabergé's London branch clients.*

above:
Silver-gilt imperial presentation case of translucent royal-
blue enamel on sunray *guilloché* ground. The cover applied
with a diamond-set imperial eagle; diamond-set thumbpiece. Original fitted red morocco case with gilt imperial
eagle.
Initials of August Hollming, Fabergé in Cyrillic. St. Petersburg 1908–17.
3½". Exhibition: "Fabergé in America"
*Presented by Nicholas II to Chief Police Inspector Henrik
Madsen during an imperial visit to Copenhagen.*

above, top:
Silver-gilt samorodok case decorated with various precious gems including round, oval, rectangular, triangular, and square cabochon and rose-cut stones.
Initials of KR in Cyrillic—possibly a Grachev case. St. Petersburg 1908–17. 4½″

above, bottom:
A gold case set on both sides with four intertwined jewel-encrusted arrows and further decorated with scattered stones. One side is set with a crowned Russian monogram. A gold garland decoration on either end surrounds the case. Cabochon ruby thumbpiece.
KFabergé in Cyrillic, imperial warrant. Moscow 1896–1908. 3⅝″. Inventory No. 26480

opposite, clockwise from top:
Two-color gold signature case, its body decorated with numerous signatures and souvenirs on front and back, including a blue enamel shield with a crown above. The border of the case is ornamented with a neo-Greek key pattern, its thumbpiece set with a cabochon sapphire.
Initials of A.B. St. Petersburg 1908–17. 3½″

A large gold case, the whole body uniformly reeded, the lid set with two intertwined monograms, a Roman figure "X," a diamond-studded cat with ruby eyes, and an inscription ("Amico"), all set with rose-cut diamonds, sapphires, and rubies. Match compartment and striker plate. Engraved inscription inside in Cyrillic.
Cabochon ruby thumbpiece.
Initials of Gabriel Niukkanen. St. Petersburg 1896–1908. 4⅜″

Silver-gilt signature case, both sides of which are decorated with various signatures and symbols in gold and enamel. On one end is a gold signature with a yellow-and-red enamel epaulette. Match compartment with outside striker plate and a place for a tinder cord.
Initials of August Hollming, Fabergé in Cyrillic. St. Petersburg 1908–17. 4″

An imperial gold presentation case with royal monograms. Its sunburst reeded body is applied on each side with a diamond or an enameled princely crown, and the lid is further set with three interlaced monograms and an imperial eagle in the middle with enameled shield on chest. Cabochon amethyst thumbpiece.
Initials of Andre Karlovich Adler. St. Petersburg 1908–17. 4″

clockwise from top:
Gold-mounted silver souvenir cigar case of rectangular shape with rounded corners. Both sides applied with two-color gold signatures, ciphers, and other symbols and, on one side, an enameled crest of the city of Riga is below an imperial crown.
N. Sн in Cyrillic—unknown maker from Riga. 5″

Silver souvenir case, the cover and back applied with gold and enamel signatures and symbols. Two signatures read "Mama," "Mavrika." Gilt interior, cabochon garnet thumbpiece.
KFABERGÉ in Cyrillic, imperial warrant. Moscow 1908–17. 4″. Inventory No. 24707

Silver signature case, both sides mounted with numerous monograms and signatures, regimental devices, enameled decorations, white enamel crosses, and the imperial eagle set with a faceted red stone. Gilt interior. Inside has Cyrillic inscription as well as the date 1908.
Initials of I. P. Sмirnov in Cyrillic. Moscow 1896–1908. 4″
The white cross is the emblem of the Corps des Pages, the prestigious imperial military and regimental academy of Russia; it is the cross of the Order of Malta, which came under Russian protection in the reign of Paul I, and is also the same shape as the cross of the Order of St. George, Imperial Russia's highest military order, seen on the lower left of the case.

A silver souvenir case, its lid engraved and decorated with numerous souvenirs including a red-and-blue enameled imperial crest. Gilt interior and cabochon ruby thumbpiece.
Initials of Pavel Ivanovich Koshelev. Moscow 1908–17. 4¼″

Personalized silver souvenir signature case, the cover applied with signatures and gold symbols. Cabochon red-stone thumbpiece.
A. Sн in Cyrillic—unknown maker. Moscow 1908–17. 4⅜″

clockwise from top:

A silver reeded case with an imperial crest in the center with dates 1914 and 1915 and numerous other symbols in gold and enamel. Interior inscription dated April 1, 1903, and a signature in Cyrillic.
Initials of S. NAZAROV. Moscow 1896–1908. 3¾"

A silver souvenir case, its lid decorated with monograms, signatures, crests, and a gold plaque of the pilsner beer trademark, Riga. Gilt interior, cabochon sapphire thumbpiece.
Initials of JB—unknown maker. 1896–1908. 4¼"

Silver case of sunburst design emanating from the cabochon ruby thumbpiece. Of rectangular shape with rounded corners and decorated with various signatures in gold, centered by a round gold plaque with an inscription in Russian reading: "Modest token of my love."
Initials of BB—unknown maker. Moscow 1896–1908. 4¼"

Silver gold-mounted souvenir case, the cover applied with a spider decorated with rose-cut diamonds, emeralds, and a large opal for the body. Further ornamented on the front and back of the case by numerous gold and enameled symbols, including a crown with seed pearls, coats of arms, bugs, and animals. Two cabochon sapphire thumbpieces.
Marks in Cyrillic of unknown maker. Moscow 1908–17. 4⅛"

clockwise from top:
Silver samorodok souvenir case, the cover applied with a Russian imperial double-headed eagle and numerous other symbols in gold and enamel. Gold-mounted cabochon sapphire thumbpiece.
Initials P.B. and F. KUROCHKINA—unknown makers. St. Petersburg 1908–17. 4″

A silver signature case with hammered body overall applied with various gold signatures, monograms, crests, and symbols in gold and enamel. Match compartment and space for tinder cord. Sapphire thumbpiece set in gold, gilt interior.
Initials of ANDERS MICKELSON. St. Petersburg pre-1896. 4″

A silver signature case, its polished body decorated with numerous enameled crests and one side with a small cameo in the corner.
Maker's initials MI in Cyrillic. St. Petersburg 1896–1908. 4⅛″

A silver signature case applied with numerous gold monograms and symbols. Gilt interior. Cabochon sapphire thumbpiece.
Unknown maker, import marks. Moscow 1908–17. 4⅛″

A silver signature case with crowned initials, monograms, and other gold and enamel mementos. Other side with monograms centered by a Russian imperial crest with the words "Livadia Palace 1809–1911" written on it and profiles of Czar Nicholas II and Czarina Alexandra. Silver thumbpiece.
IVAN KHLEBNIKOV. Moscow pre-1896. 3¾″

A polished silver case centered with a reeded cross enameled with blue and white; top right corner is set with an enameled shield further set with a gold signature and an inscribed circle in the top left. Silver thumbpiece.
Initials RP—unknown Moscow maker. 1896–1908. 4½″

A silver samorodok case. Its lid is decorated with a double-headed eagle in the top left corner, a large gold crowned monogram in the top right corner, other symbols in gold and enamel, and busts of the Czar and Czarina. Oval silver-set turquoise thumbpiece.
Initials AO—unknown maker. Moscow 1908–17. 4″

A silver signature case with numerous gold monograms, crests, epaulettes, and other applied gold and silver mementos centered by a jeton of the Grand Duke Michael Artillery School. On the back is a gold signature monogram. Silver thumbpiece.
Moscow Society of Jewelers. Moscow 1896–1908. 4⅛″

center top:
A large polished gold souvenir case centered with a miniature of Peter the Great on horseback, further decorated on both sides with numerous gold monograms and symbols in gold and enamel. Cabochon sapphire thumbpiece.
FEDOR LORIE. Moscow 1908–17. 4½″

center bottom:
A silver and enamel case. The lid is enameled with a queen of diamonds, and the reverse is enameled blue in a geometric cane pattern.
Initials possibly of VASILY SEMYONOV, assay maker B.C. 1871. Moscow pre-1896. 3½″

clockwise from top:

A silver souvenir case, its body reeded at 45 degrees. The lid is decorated with numerous souvenirs and monograms. Gilt interior and silver thumbpiece.

Initials of I. P. SMIRNOV in Cyrillic. Moscow pre-1896. 3½″

A silver souvenir case, its lid decorated with numerous gold symbols in gold and enamel. Reverse centered with St. George slaying the dragon in silver with an imperial crown above and in inscription in Cyrillic. The inside is also engraved in Cyrillic with the date August 13, 1915. Cabochon ruby thumbpiece set in gold.

Moscow Society of Jewelers. Moscow 1908–17. 4½″

A large silver case, both sides decorated with numerous crests and symbols. Match compartment and place for tinder cord. Lid of match case (on end) has a gun, wheat stalks, and head of hunting dog set with a diamond eye.

Moscow Society of Jewelers. Moscow 1908–17. 5″

A silver signature case with two reeded borders, both sides decorated with numerous signatures in gold. One side centered with a crest with turquoise-blue enamel, and the other has diamond and pearls set within a decoration.

Moscow Society of Jewelers. Moscow 1896–1908. 4½″

A silver souvenir case, both sides decorated with large stylized monograms, signatures in gold, and other symbols. Cabochon sapphire thumbpiece.

Initials of JB—unknown maker. Moscow 1896–1908. 4⅛″

center:

A silver souvenir case of slightly curved section. Both sides are decorated with gold, silver, enamel, and gem-set military badges, signatures, and symbols. Gold-enameled pendant miniature epaulettes (several of which are engraved) suspended on chains from one corner.

Initials of A. FULD. Moscow pre-1896. 3¾″

opposite, clockwise from top left:
Silver-gilt presentation case with a Russian imperial crest on the lid, along with several signatures and monograms, and cabochon sapphire thumbpiece. On the back, more signatures, double eagle, a protruding cross, a cat with arched back, and a long leaf with a row of diamonds up the center. "Sofia" on plaque.
KFABERGÉ in Cyrillic with imperial warrant. Moscow 1896–1908. 3⅞"

A large silver signature case centered with gold intertwined monogram consisting of two letters in Cyrillic—AO—further decorated with numerous other signatures in gold and dated 1883–1908. The reverse, shown here, is similarly decorated, and is also applied with a Russian blue, white, and red flag in enamel. Gilt interior. Cabochon red stone thumbpiece.
Initials of SPE in Cyrillic—unknown maker. Moscow 1896–1908. 4⅛"

Silver souvenir case applied with enameled charms and numerous gold monograms and signatures and centered with an oval portrait. Scattered with cabochon stones. Silver thumbpiece. Gilt interior.
Initials of JN—unknown maker. St. Petersburg pre-1896. 3½"

Signatures include those of Fabergé workmaster J. V. Aarne, the Bremen shipowner and porcelain collector Ernst Blohm, O. Pettersson, and Marakalli, and the date 18. XII. 1904.

A silver case. Its lid decorated with gold butterfly in the left corner, the other side decorated with a Russian stamp enameled over two postal franks dated 1897, and the back engraved with a gold signature. Gilt interior. Cabochon sapphire thumbpiece set in silver.
3¼"
Two postage stamps identical to the one on the cover are on the inside of the case.

A small silver coin purse engraved with a floral motif and further applied with gold and enameled mementos on front and back. Inside has three blue satin sections. Silver thumbpiece.
Initials of FEODOR AFANASSIEV. 1896–1908. 2¾"

above, clockwise from top left:
An unusual gunmetal case, the body decorated with rose-cut diamonds, and a rose-cut diamond thumbpiece. The reverse has a monogram. The gold trim inside bears the inscription "22-4-1910."
Initials of ANDERS NEVALAINEN. Moscow 1908–17. 3⅞"

Gunmetal case designed with red and yellow gold samorodok effect. The cover is set with a scattered ruby, sapphire, diamond, and emerald with cabochon sapphire thumbpiece.
3⅞"

A jeweled gold-and-gunmetal case with rounded corners. The lid is applied with the Russian imperial double-headed eagle centered with a red stone. Gold engraved borders and chased foliate thumbpiece.
3⅝"

opposite:
Case of silver-gilt and *guilloché* purple enamel over moiré ground. Oblong with rounded corners, and a two-color gold-chased laurel band on either end, with match compartment and parcel-gilt and rose-cut diamond thumbpiece.
Initials of HENRIK WIGSTRÖM, FABERGÉ, CF, London import marks. St. Petersburg 1908–17. 3⅜″. Inventory No. 22275

above:
Silver-gilt and evening-blue enamel over wavy engine-turned lady's case with match compartment, the margins bound by raised laurel-leaf bands. In original fitted wooden case with the list of Fabergé branches open at the time—St. Petersburg, Moscow, London—inscribed inside. Diamond-set thumbpiece.

Inscription inside in script: *"Je vous remercie du fond du coeur, Pour toutes vos bontés cher ami, Je prierai Dieu que chaque heure soit, pour vous, une heure bénie.*
H.F.
from
h.de.S.
Harrogate 1915"
("I thank you from the bottom of my heart, for all your kindness, dear friend, I will pray to God that each hour will be, for you, a blessed one").
Initials of HENRIK WIGSTRÖM, FABERGÉ, CF, London import marks for 1914. St. Petersburg 1908–17. 3⅜″. Inventory No. 24691. Exhibition: "Carl Fabergé: Goldsmith to the Tsar"
According to the Fabergé London sales ledger, inventory #24691, a cigarette case in "steel blue enamel" was sold for £23 on 24 December 1915 to a Mrs. Farquharson.

opposite:
A silver-gilt case whose entire body is decorated with deep green *guilloché* enamel on moiré ground. The lid is centered with a gold five-ruble piece dated 1779 and a profile of Catherine the Great in diamond surround. Thumbpiece set with a row of rose-cut diamonds. Other side of coin can be seen from inside the lid.
Initials of AUGUST HOLLMING, FABERGÉ in Cyrillic. St. Petersburg 1908–17.
3⅞". Inventory No. 24808
Featured on the Fabergé Arts Foundation Christmas card, 1996.

above:
A silver-gilt and enamel case decorated with opaque turquoise, enamel stripes within two mauve enameled bands. The cover is set with a gold Empress Elizabeth I one-ruble coin dated 1756 within rose-cut diamond surround. Diamond thumbpiece. Fitted case.
Initials of HENRIK WIGSTRÖM, FABERGÉ in Cyrillic. St. Petersburg 1896–1908. 3⅞"

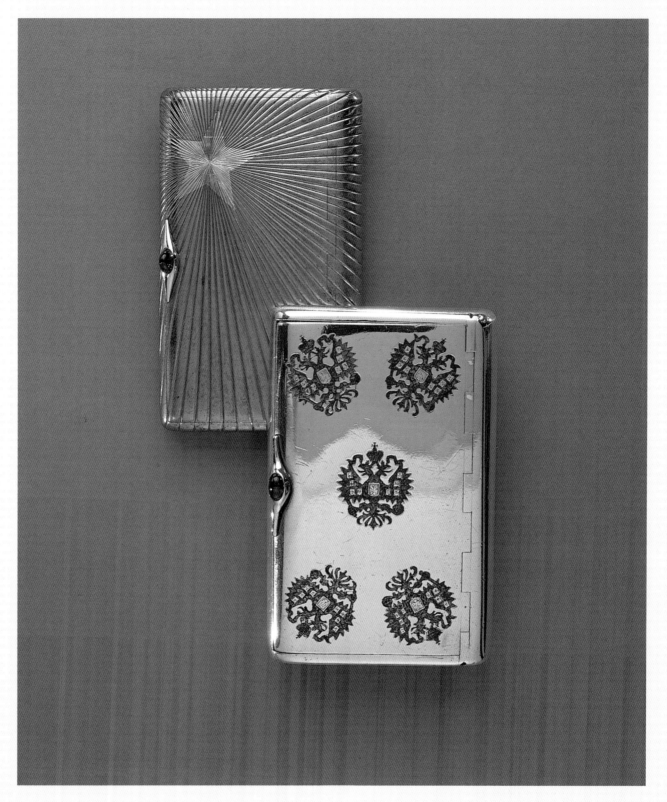

top:
A silver case of oval section, decorated with a sunburst
pattern emanating from a gold five-pointed star, with
cabochon sapphire thumbpiece. Match compartment and
space for tinder cord.
Initials of FRIEDRICH KOECHLI. St. Petersburg pre-1896. 3⅞″

bottom:
A silver case, its body decorated on both sides with iron
double-headed eagles set flush into the surface. Interior
inscribed "To Mirokhanovsky from the commander of the
Imperial Guard Preobrazhensky Regiment of His Imperial
Highness Grand Duke Konstantin Konstantinovich."
Cabochon sapphire thumbpiece.
Initials of GD in Cyrillic. St. Petersburg 1896–1908. 3⅞″

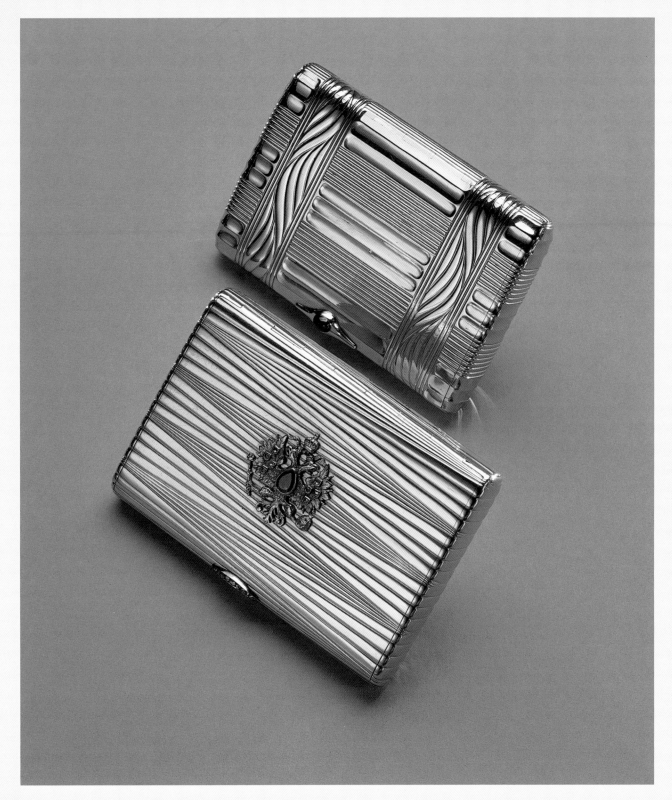

top:
A gold case. The entire body is reeded with alternating bands of wide and narrow red gold. Both ends of the case are decorated with two perpendicular bands containing a swirl design. Cabochon sapphire thumbpiece.
Initials of ALBERT HOLMSTRÖM. St. Petersburg 1908–17. 3¾″. Exhibition: "Fabergé and Finland"

bottom:
A gold imperial presentation case with fluted reed design. The lid is set with a Russian double-headed eagle decorated with a large ruby in the center and eight small rose-cut diamonds. Thumbpiece is decorated with a row of rose-cut diamonds.
Initials of AUGUST HOLLMING, KFABERGÉ in Cyrillic. St. Petersburg 1908–17. 4″. Inventory No. 24376. Exhibition: "Fabergé and Finland"

above:
Unusual concave silver-gilt and gold case decorated with
translucent oyster-white enamel over moiré *guilloché*
ground. Its lid is further ornamented with an *en plein*
princely crest of the Demidoff family, princes of San
Donato. Gold leaf borders and gold thumbpiece.
Initials of HENRIK WIGSTRÖM, FABERGÉ in Cyrillic. St. Petersburg
1896–1908. 3⅛″

opposite:
Gilded silver and royal-blue enamel presentation case, the
cover set with the Russian imperial eagle in diamonds and
with a diamond-row thumbpiece. Fitted royal presentation
box. The interior bears the Cyrillic inscription
"Presentation of His Majesty to Prince N.A. Kudashev"
and is dated 23 January 1915.
Initials of AUGUST HOLLMING, FABERGÉ in Cyrillic. St. Petersburg 1908–17.
3¹⁵⁄₁₆″. Exhibitions: "Fabergé"; "Treasures of Fabergé"
*Prince Kudashev was an official of the Hermitage. He foresaw
the dangers of the coming revolution and got both his family and
his wealth to Paris within two years of receiving this case, just
on the eve of the revolution.*

inset: Interior detail

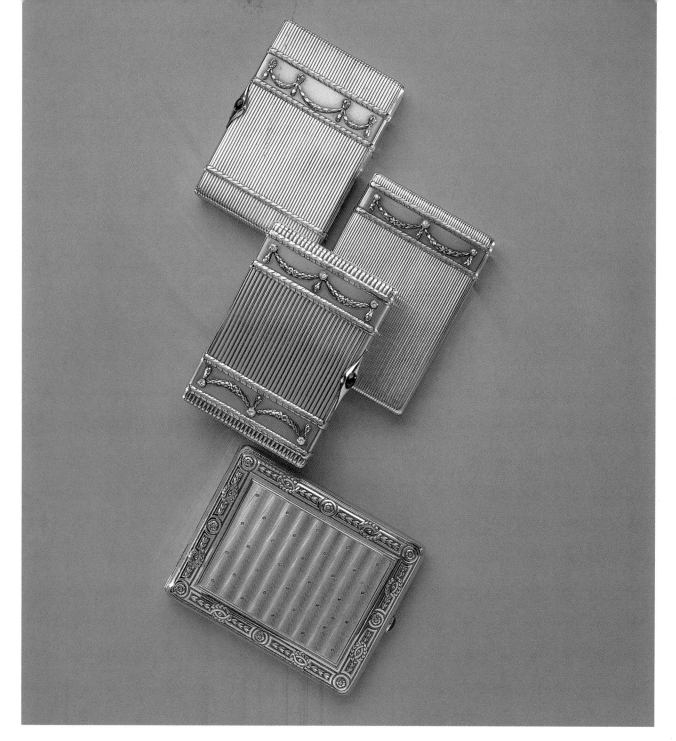

above, top to bottom:
A Russian two-color gold case. Its entire
body is reeded, and the left part is decorated with a matte gold panel with laurel-
leaf borders, containing ribbon swags.
Cabochon sapphire thumbpiece.
Initials of JAKOV ROSEN. St. Petersburg 1908–17. 3⅞″.

A three-color gold case. Its entire body is
reeded, and the upper part is decorated
with laurel-leaf borders containing a garland set with rose-cut diamonds. Rose-cut
diamond thumbpiece.
Initials of JAKOV ROSEN. St. Petersburg 1908–17. 3⅞″.

Red-and-green-gold reeded case with two
matte bands within chased green-gold
palmette borders and applied with ribbon-
tied laurel-leaf swags suspended from
circular-cut diamonds. Cabochon sapphire
thumbpiece.
Initials of JAKOV ROSEN. St. Petersburg 1908–17. 3⅞″.

Large and unusual two-color gold case in
the Louis XVI style with a cabochon ruby
thumbpiece. The body of the case is
engine turned in a pattern of waves and
pellets within a floral border.
Initials of HENRIK WIGSTRÖM, FABERGÉ in Cyrillic.
St. Petersburg 1896–1908. 4⅛″. Inventory No. 17765.
Exhibition: "Fabergé in America"

opposite:
Two-color pink *guilloché* enamel and
diamond-set case with a circular design on
top and bottom with acanthus-leaf
borders. Two panels of darker pink at
either end. Large faceted diamond
thumbpiece. Contained in the original
fitted case.
Initials of CARL HAHN. St. Petersburg pre-1896. 3½″.

opposite, clockwise from top:
Two-color gold case, the sides decorated in the Renaissance style with mythical birds perched on scrolling foliage and a cartouche engraved in yellow gold on a pink sable gold ground, with cabochon sapphire thumbpiece.
Initials of OSKAR PIHL, imperial warrant. Moscow pre-1896. 3⅜". Inventory No. 4803.
Exhibition: "Fabergé in America"
A rarely seen workmaster, Pihl was the father of Alma Pihl, who became a major designer with Fabergé in St. Petersburg. She designed the snowflake pieces and two imperial eggs.

A silver and two-color gold case, its body chased and engraved with silver-gilt sycamore seeds in the Japanese style.
Initials of G. D. St. Petersburg 1896–1908. 3⅞"

A gold imperial presentation case decorated with applied strapwork, the cover with an imperial double-headed eagle. Cabochon sapphire thumbpiece between two diamonds. Interior contains an ivory plaque.
Ivory plaque: Heading:
MILITARY ATTACHE TO THE
IMPERIAL RUSSIAN EMBASSY
2 WHITEHALL COURT.
S.W.
"Sir, I am commanded by His Imperial Majesty the Emperor of Russia, my August Master, to forward to you the inclosed [sic] golden cigarette case. His Majesty desires you to accept it as a present in acknowledgment of services

rendered by you to some of His Majesty's subjects on the occasion of their visit to this country during the summer of 1910. I remain, Sir, your obedient servant.
N. Golyernsiu
Lieutenant Colonel
Sir Arthur Trevor Dawson
2 Green Street
London W.
St. Petersburg 1908–17. 3⅞"
The case was presented to Sir Arthur Dawson circa 1910.

above: Interior detail

clockwise from top:

An octagonal silver case, its lid decorated with a large repoussé Russian double-headed eagle with St. George and the Dragon within a shield. Gilt interior.

4⅛″

A polished silver case centered with large repoussé and chased Russian double-headed eagle with extended wings. Gilt interior.

4″

A silver case. Its lid is decorated with a silver double-headed eagle and a multicolored enamel map of Europe superimposed on its chest. Engraved inside on both sides with a shield and an illegible name and dated December 12–25 1915. Match compartment. Cabochon sapphire thumbpiece.

Initials of ANDERS NEVALAINEN, KFABERGÉ in Cyrillic, imperial warrant. St. Petersburg 1896–1908. 3⅞″. Inventory No. 8681

Silver imperial presentation case with a gilt interior. The entire lid is repoussé with a Russian double-headed eagle and further chased with foliate motif in the corners. Thumbpiece is set with a cabochon sapphire.

KFABERGÉ in Cyrillic, imperial warrant. Moscow 1908–17. 3⅞″

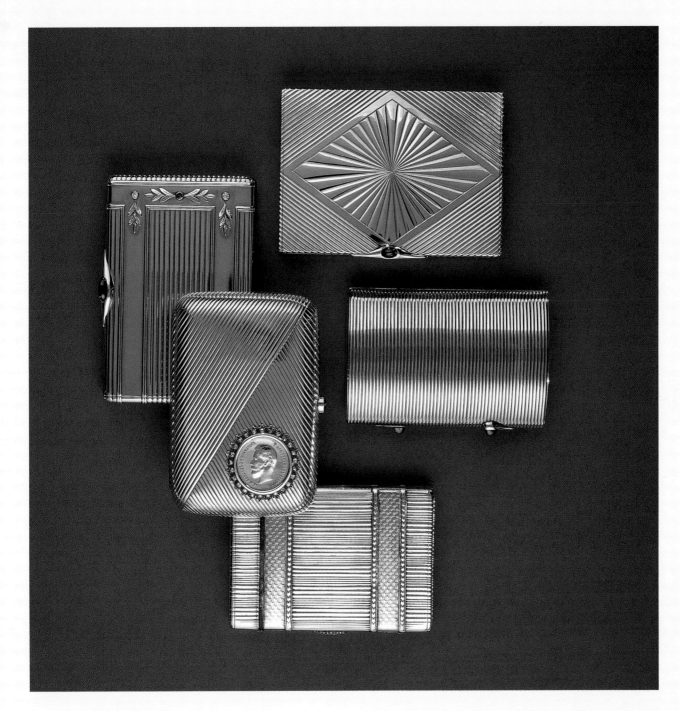

clockwise from top:

A polished gold case, both sides of which are decorated with flutes emanating from the center creating a sort of diamond geometric pattern with diagonally ribbed corners. Cabochon sapphire thumbpiece.
Initials of IVAN ZAKHAROV. Moscow 1908–17. 3⅞″

Gold ribbed case of convex shape. Double sapphire thumbpieces.
KFABERGÉ in Cyrillic, imperial warrant. Moscow pre-1896. 3½″. Inventory No. 12707

A gold rectangular case. Its entire body is reeded, with two engine-turned bands bordered by leaf tips. Diamond-set thumbpiece.
Initials of AUGUST HOLLMING, FABERGÉ in Cyrillic. St. Petersburg 1896–1908. 3½″

A gold case, its reeded lid decorated with a Russian gold coin with the profile of Nicholas II set in the lower right corner within a row of rose-cut diamonds. Inside is an inscription reading "Presented to Lieut. J. C. Harrison Scott Grey by H.M. the Emperor of Russia on the occasion of his commanding the escort of His Majesty, Ballater to Balmoral Sept. 22, Balmoral to Ballater Oct. 3, 1896."
Initials of VICTOR AARNE. St. Petersburg pre-1896. 3⅝″. Exhibition: "Fabergé in America"
The case was presented to the British escort officer on the occasion of the state visit of Czar Nicholas II, Czarina Alexandra Feodorovna, and their first child, Olga, to Queen Victoria in Balmoral following their coronation in 1896.

A two-color gold case with a match compartment, its lid decorated with a narrow reeded panel in the center and two narrow panels on the edges. Also applied with laurel branches embellished with two rose-cut diamonds and one sapphire. Cabochon sapphire thumbpiece.
Initials of JAKOV ROSEN. St. Petersburg 1908–17. 3⅞″

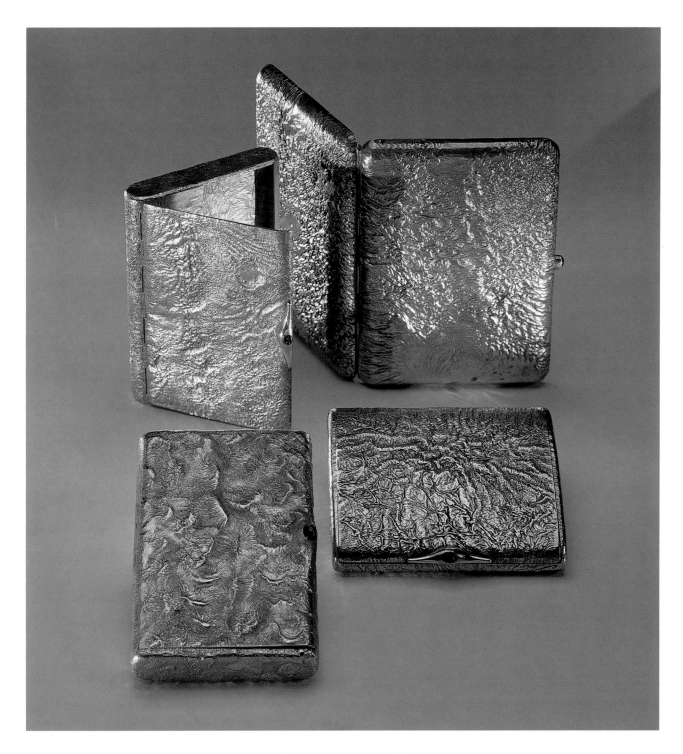

opposite, top:
A jeweled gold presentation samorodok case. Its lid is applied with a Russian imperial crest with diamonds. Cabochon sapphire thumbpiece set in red gold.
Ivan Morozov, imperial warrant. St. Petersburg, 1908–17. 3⅞″

below:
Gold samorodok imperial presentation case of rectangular section, the lid applied with an imperial eagle set with a diamond. Cabochon sapphire thumbpiece.
Initials of YS—maker in Odessa. Odessa 1908–17. 4″

above, clockwise from top right:
Silver-gilt samorodok case with cabochon sapphire thumbpiece mounted in silver.
Odessa 1908–17. 4⅛″

Silver-gilt samorodok case decorated with cabochon sapphire thumbpiece set in silver.
Initials of Julius Rappoport, Fabergé in Cyrillic. St. Petersburg 1908–17. 3⅞″

A gold samorodok case. Cabochon sapphire thumbpiece.
Initials of August Hollming, Fabergé in Cyrillic. St. Petersburg 1908–17. 4″

A gold samorodok case. Cabochon sapphire thumbpiece.
Initials of Karl Gustav Johansson Lundell. St. Petersburg 1908–17. 3¾″

clockwise from top:

Gilded silver samorodok case, the cover applied with a gold imperial eagle. Cabochon sapphire thumbpiece. In the original red leather case with imperial eagle on the cover. With presentation letter to A. Beal dated 1911: "I am desired by Prince Obolensky, on behalf of The Empress of Russia, to send you the enclosed silver case, as a Souvenir of Her Imperial Majesty's recent visit to England.
Yours faithfully, T. Gordon Watson."
KFABERGÉ in Cyrillic, imperial warrant. Moscow 1908–17. 3⅞″

A silver samorodok case with a match compartment and tinder cord. Cabochon sapphire thumbpiece. The inside cover is engraved with a noble crest and *"In steter Dankbarkeit, Hans-Tochen 18-6-18"* ("With gratitude, Hans Tochen, 18 June, 1918").
Initials of ANDERS NEVALAINEN, KFABERGÉ in Cyrillic, imperial warrant. St. Petersburg pre-1896. 4⅜″. Inventory No. 4030. Exhibition: "Fabergé and Finland"

Silver samorodok case with colored stones, both faceted and cabochon, that were added later. Cabochon sapphire thumbpiece.
Initials of ANDERS NEVALAINEN, KFABERGÉ in Cyrillic, imperial warrant. 3⅞″

clockwise from top:
A silver samorodok case. Its lid is decorated with a double-headed eagle with shield, two black enameled epaulettes, a circular emblem inscribed in Russian ("Be Lucky"), and other monograms and symbols. Cabochon sapphire thumbpiece. Inscription on edge showing the date 1917.
4½″

Silver samorodok rectangular cigarette case in the Art Nouveau style, the textured surface repoussé with the faces of a man and a woman. Set with a green cabochon thumbpiece.
Odessa 1908–17. 4½″

Silver samorodok case, the lid applied with various emblems in enamel. Gold-set cabochon sapphire thumbpiece. Gilded interior.
Initials of AUGUST HOLLMING, FABERGÉ in Cyrillic. St. Petersburg 1908–17. 3⅞″

A silver samorodok case with gilt interior. Surface shows pronounced mounds of silver in abstract design.
Initials of IVAN SALTIKOV. MOSCOW 1908–17. 4½″

above, clockwise from top:
An elongated silver samorodok case with
cabochon sapphire thumbpiece.
Initials of AUGUST HOLLMING. St. Petersburg 1908–17. 6″

Silver samorodok cigarette case. Silver
thumbpiece set with a cabochon sapphire.
Gilt interior.
Initials of JULIUS RAPPOPORT, FABERGÉ in Cyrillic.
St. Petersburg 1908–17. 4″

Silver samorodok case with gilt interior
and silver-mounted amethyst thumbpiece.
Maker's mark in Cyrillic of unknown Soviet maker.
St. Petersburg 1908–17. 3¾″

opposite:
Gold samorodok case randomly decorated
with several gems, including two diamonds, two emeralds, two rubies, and a
cabochon sapphire thumbpiece.
Initials of AUGUST HOLLMING, FABERGÉ in Cyrillic.
St. Petersburg 1908–17. 3½″. Inventory No. 21816

above:
Silver-gilt gold-mounted case of oval section with translucent salmon-colored enamel over waved *guilloché* ground,
the gold borders chased with acanthus leaves. Diamond
thumbpiece.
Initials of HENRIK WIGSTRÖM, FABERGÉ in Cyrillic. St. Petersburg 1908–17.
4″. Inventory No. 26744
*This color is similar to the "Sevres" pink of the French royal
porcelain.*

opposite:
A silver-gilt and gold white *guilloché* enamel cigarette case
over sunburst ground. Match compartment with striker
plate, and white opalescent *guilloché* enamel cigarette holder inside. Rose-cut diamond thumbpiece.
Initials of AUGUST HOLLMING, FABERGÉ in Cyrillic. St. Petersburg 1908–17.
3⅛″

Silver-gilt case with alternating blue and ivory translucent enamel stripes over *guilloché* ground. Diamond thumbpiece.
Initials of August Holmström, Fabergé in Cyrillic. St. Petersburg pre-1896. 3⅛″. Exhibition: "Fabergé and Finland"
Fabergé traditionally made pieces in these colors—the racing colors of the Rothschild horses—for the Rothschild family.

left:
A gold case, its entire body engine turned, both sides
decorated with dark blue enamel stripes, the edges with a
white enamel key pattern. Thumbpiece set with rose-cut
diamonds.
Initials of Henrik Wigström. St. Petersburg 1908–17. 3⁷⁄₁₆″. Inventory No.
25773. Exhibition: "Great Fabergé in the Hermitage"

right:
Gold engine-turned enameled case decorated with white
enamel stripes and borders of a neo-Greek key pattern in
blue enamel. Diamond-set thumbpiece.
Initials of Henrik Wigström, Fabergé, English import marks.
St. Petersburg 1908–17. 3⅜″. Inventory No. 25616. Exhibition: "Fabergé in
America"
*The interior of the case is inscribed with a presentation message
from Barbara Hutton to Cary Grant on the occasion of his
birthday: "Merci February 18, 1942."*

top to bottom:

An imperial presentation case in gold and nephrite, decorated with a large double-headed eagle set with rubies and diamonds. Ruby thumbpiece.
Initials of Henrik Wigström, Fabergé in Cyrillic. St. Petersburg 1896–1908. 3⅞″. Exhibitions: "Fabergé and Finland"; "Fabergé: Loistavaa Kultasepäntaidetta"

Gold and nephrite case applied with a gold Russian imperial double-headed eagle with a square diamond in the center. Cabochon sapphire thumbpiece.
Initials of Michael Perchin, Fabergé in Cyrillic. 1896–1908. 3½″

Nephrite and gold-mounted case with a Russian imperial double-headed eagle in silver decorated with rose-cut diamonds.
Initials of August Hollming, Fabergé in Cyrillic. St. Petersburg 1908–17. 3⅞″

clockwise from top left:

A nephrite case in a red gold mount, decorated with opaque white enamel stripes and set with eight small cabochon rubies, separated by green-gold laurel.

Initials of HENRIK WIGSTRÖM, FABERGÉ in Cyrillic. St. Petersburg 1896–1908. 3⅜″. Inventory No. 17072

A jeweled, trunk-shaped nephrite box, oblong with rounded sides. The clasp and hinges are of gold and platinum with interlaced diamond bands set with cabochon rubies.

Initials of C.F. 3⅛″

A tubular gold and nephrite cigarette-holder box (with the cigarette-holder inside). Decorated with a row of rose-cut diamonds.

3″. Inventory No. 24051

above, clockwise from top:
A nephrite presentation case mounted
with gold, the lid applied with a
roundel of pink *guilloché* enamel with a
crowned Cyrillic monogram, "MP."
The reverse of the roundel etched with
"XXV." Diamond thumbpiece.
Initials of Henrik Wigström, Fabergé in Cyrillic.
St. Petersburg 1896–1908. 3⅞". Exhibition:
"Fabergé in America"
*A twenty-fifth wedding anniversary gift,
probably to Grand Duchess Maria
Pavlovna, wife of Duke Vladimir, in 1899.*

Carved nephrite case. The cover and
base are applied with swags of green-
gold berried leafage pendant from red-
gold ribbons. Cabochon emerald
thumbpiece.
Initials KF in Cyrillic. Moscow pre-1896. 3⅞".
Inventory No. 15726. Exhibition: "Fabergé in
America"

A gold and nephrite case. Its lid is
applied with a jeweled basket of flowers within a jeweled wreath of flowers,
the gold rim with diamond-set ribbons.
Flowers set with rubies, diamonds, and
emeralds. Amethyst thumbpiece.
1908–17. 4⅛"

opposite:
Carved nephrite case of elephants with
ruby eyes, with gold mountings and
cabochon ruby thumbpiece.
KFabergé in Cyrillic. St. Petersburg 1908–17. 3¾"

clockwise from top:

A large two-color gold case of fluted design decorated on one side (not shown) with a centered coat of arms with a helmet, a blue enameled shield with a crescent, a log, and a six-pointed star, all surrounded with floral motif in blue enamel. On the cover are the dates 1857–1905 and a crowned initial. Interior inscribed with the names of forty-two of Albedyll's colleagues. Cabochon sapphire thumbpiece.
ALEXANDER TILLANDER. St. Petersburg 1896–1908. 4″
The case was presented to Baron Theodor (Feodor Konstantinovich) Albedyll, whose family crest is shown on the back. He is from an old Baltic noble family.

An imperial red and yellow gold fluted case in sunburst pattern emanating from a central dark blue enamel monogram of Grand Duke Nicholas Nicholaevich in diamond surround. Cabochon sapphire thumbpiece.
Initials of AUGUST HOLLMING, FABERGÉ in Cyrillic. St. Petersburg 1908–17. 3½″
Presented by Czar Nicholas II to his cousin Grand Duke Nicholas Nicholaevich. Grandson of Czar Nicholas I, he was commander in chief of the Russian army during 1914 and 1915. He escaped from Russia and died in the Côte d'Azur in 1929.

Two-color gold case decorated with four red and yellow gold reeded triangles. The cover has an applied monogram "MM" in white, red, and blue enamel below an imperial crown. Ruby thumbpiece.
Initials of ANDREI BRAGIN. St. Petersburg 1896–1908.
4″
The monogram is that of Grand Duke Michael Michaelovich, who was exiled to England in connection with his morganatic marriage. The Fabergé collection inherited by his daughter, Lady Zia Wernher, was once exhibited at Luton Hoo outside of London, the former estate and museum of Lady Zia's descendants.

clockwise from top:
Silver and gold-mounted cigarette case, with sunray pattern emanating from an applied gold imperial eagle set with an old mine-cut diamond. The thumbpiece is set with a cabochon moonstone. In original leather presentation case.
Initials of N.P. or M.P. in Cyrillic. St. Petersburg 1908–17. 3⅞″
Purported to have been presented by Nicholas II to the colonel-in-chief of the Pavlovsk Palace Guard.

A polished silver case. Its lid is decorated with a jeweled monogram "EG" underneath a crown. Match compartment, black cord with tassel.
Initials of NICHOLS and PLINCKE. St. Petersburg pre-1896. 4⅛″

A silver fluted case with a match compartment and place for a tinder cord. The lid is decorated with a gold double-headed Russian imperial eagle centered by a faceted rose-cut diamond. Cabochon sapphire thumbpiece.
Initials of PJS, unknown workmaster. St. Petersburg 1908–17. 4″. Inventory No. 9870

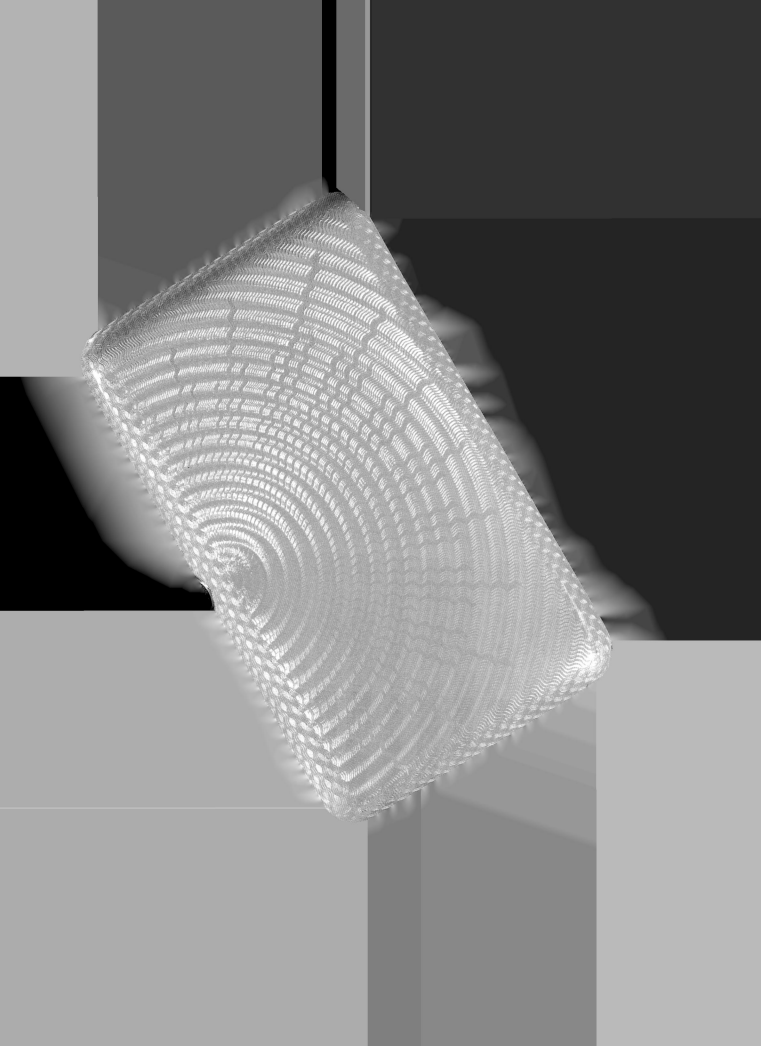

opposite:
Brilliant yellow-enamel case in sunburst pattern.
Cabochon sapphire thumbpiece.
Initials of AUGUST HOLLMING, FABERGÉ in Cyrillic. St. Petersburg
1896–1908. 3⅞″

above:
A rectangular gem-set and enameled gold-mounted
bowenite case with rounded corners. The hinged cover
mount enameled with translucent red ovals alternating
with white pellets. Green diamond thumbpiece.
Initials of MICHAEL PERCHIN, FABERGÉ in Cyrillic. St. Petersburg pre-1896.
3⅜″. Inventory No. 49127

A rock crystal case with jeweled gold mounts, of upright oval section, the entire body of rock crystal, the gold
mounts set with a band of rubies between diamond-set borders.
Initials of Henrik Wigström, CF, London marks for 1911. 3⅜". Inventory No. 59513
London ledgers indicate this case was sold to the Rothschilds on December 27, 1912.

top:
A two-color gold carved citrine case of oval section
mounted with white enamel bands decorated with green
enamel leaves. Cabochon sapphire thumbpiece.
Initials of MICHAEL PERCHIN. St. Petersburg pre-1896. 3⅜″

bottom:
A gold-mounted tortoiseshell case decorated with a cabochon sapphire thumbpiece.
Initials of MICHAEL PERCHIN, FABERGÉ in Cyrillic. St. Petersburg pre-1896.
3½″. Inventory No. 603 4B

clockwise from top:

A silver case. Its entire body is decorated with alternating bands of narrow reeding and laurel leaves. Match compartment with striker plate. Cabochon sapphire thumbpiece.

Initials of AUGUST HOLLMING, FABERGÉ in Cyrillic, CF, import marks. St. Petersburg 1908–17. 3⅜″

Silver case with reeded rectangular body; the lid is applied with the interlaced initials "H. J. K." Gilt interior, cabochon sapphire thumbpiece.

FABERGÉ in Cyrillic, FABERGÉ initials KF in Cyrillic. St. Petersburg 1908–17. 3⅜″

A silver reeded tubular case.

Initials of AUGUST HOLLMING, FABERGÉ in Cyrillic. St. Petersburg 1908–17. 3⅜″

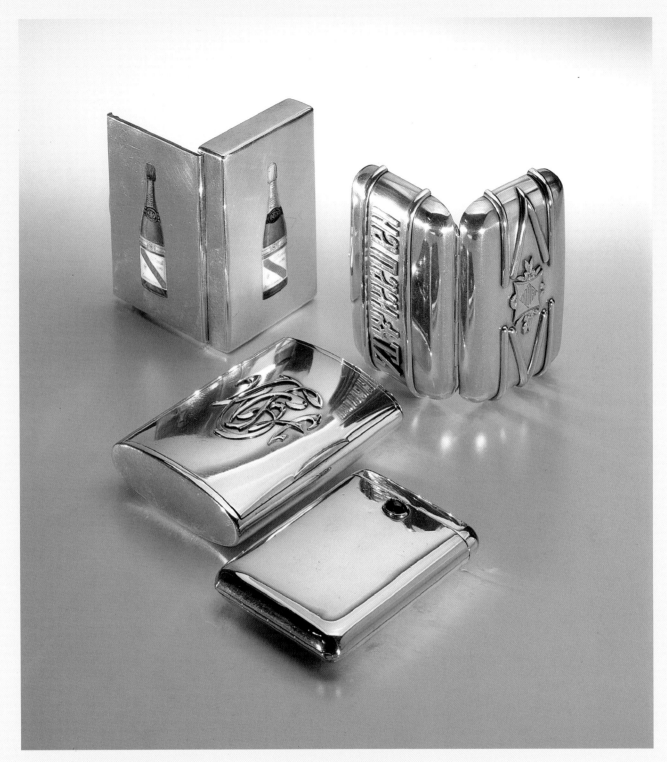

clockwise from top:

Case with enameled champagne bottles on either side: Cordon Vert, Cordon Rouge. Silver thumbpiece. Engraved signature inside.
KFABERGÉ in Cyrillic, imperial warrant. Moscow 1908–17. 3⅝″

A polished silver case decorated with a raised inscription in Russian, "With Fond Memories." The other side is set with an engraved plaque. The inside is engraved "Harry A. Ostroll New York." Silver thumbpiece.
Initials of ERIK KOLLIN, dated 1873. St. Petersburg pre-1896. 3⅝″
Erik Kollin's mark is rarely seen.

A polished silver case with a large cabochon sapphire thumbpiece in the middle which, once depressed, opens a spring-loaded upper lid. French inscription in raised gold on the back:
"Ah! qu'c'est bon l'amour"
("Ah! Love is grand").
KFABERGÉ in Cyrillic, imperial warrant. Moscow 1896–1908. 3⅝″

Silver cigarette case of oval rectangular form. The lid is applied with gold interlaced initials "HM" in Cyrillic. Gilt interior.
KFABERGÉ in Cyrillic, imperial warrant. Moscow pre-1896. 4″. Inventory No. 8851

above, clockwise from top:
Silver-gilt Art Nouveau case repoussé with poppies decorated with cabochon sapphires and a faceted diamond on the cover. Cabochon sapphire thumbpiece. Interior inscription in English script: "Edward G. Pease, Dayton, Ohio U.S.A."
KFABERGÉ in Cyrillic, imperial warrant. Moscow 1896–1908. 3⅞″. Exhibition: "Great Fabergé in the Hermitage"
This box was presented by Nicholas II in appreciation for special iron construction work in Russia to Edward G. Pease of Dayton, Ohio. When inherited by Judge Pease, it was released for sale.

Silver case chased and repoussé with an iris, stems, and leaves in the Art Nouveau style, with gilt interior and cabochon sapphire thumbpiece.
KFABERGÉ in Cyrillic, imperial warrant. Moscow pre-1896. 4¼″

Silver jeweled case. The cover is designed as a foliate cluster enhanced with an oval emerald cabochon and tapering lines of rose-cut diamonds. Sapphire cabochon thumbpiece.
KFABERGÉ in Cyrillic, imperial warrant. Moscow 1896–1908. 3⅞″. Inventory No. 93175

Silver case repoussé and chased with scrolls and neo-rococo shellwork with gilt interior. Reverse inscribed in Cyrillic: "To Dear Surgeon M. Berger from A. Karasik for Saving My Life, 22 VI-51."
KFABERGÉ in Cyrillic, imperial warrant. Moscow pre-1896; also bearing later marks for 1908–17. 3⅞″

opposite:
A silver imperial presentation case set with a gold Russian imperial crest on the cover and decorated with wheat stalks. Cabochon sapphire thumbpiece. Fitted case.
KFABERGÉ in Cyrillic, imperial warrant. Moscow 1896–1908. 3⅞″. Inventory No. 14379

clockwise from top:

Two-color gold case decorated with alternating yellow and wide red-gold bands. The cover is applied with an imperial double-headed eagle with coat of arms. Cabochon sapphire thumbpiece.
Initials of Albert Holmström, Fabergé in Cyrillic. St. Petersburg 1908–17. 3¾″. Inventory No. 25880

Ribbed gold case with match compartment and original tinder cord in the colors of the Order of St. George. The entire surface of the case is decorated with alternating reeded and etched bands. Rose-cut diamond thumbpiece.
Initials of August Hollming, Fabergé in Cyrillic, CF, import marks. St. Petersburg 1908–17. 3⅝″. Inventory No. 21689

Gold concave case decorated with alternating bands of wide and narrow reeding. Cabochon sapphire thumbpiece.
Fabergé in Cyrillic, KF in Cyrillic. St. Petersburg 1908–17. 3⅝″. Inventory No. 25977

A gold reeded imperial presentation case. The cover is set with a diamond-studded double-headed eagle. Cabochon sapphire thumbpiece.
Initials of Gabriel Niukkanen. St. Petersburg 1896–1908. 3¾″. Inventory No. 592 E

left to right:
Three-color gold case with stripes of alternating colors. Row of rose-cut diamonds thumbpiece.
Initials of HENRIK WIGSTRÖM. St. Petersburg 1908–17. 3½″

A two-color gold case with alternating etched stripes of green and red gold and opaque white enamel.
Initials of HENRIK WIGSTRÖM, FABERGÉ in Cyrillic. St. Petersburg 1908–17. 3½″. Inventory No. 2341E

Cylindrical gold-ribbed match case. The cover is decorated with a large cabochon chalcedony in rose-cut diamond surround, with circular-cut diamond pushpiece. The base has a striker plate.
Initials of ERIK KOLLIN, FABERGÉ in Cyrillic. St. Petersburg pre-1896. 1¾″

top to bottom:

Birchwood case with gold trim and cabochon sapphire thumbpiece.
Initials of Alfred Thielemann. St. Petersburg
pre-1896. 3½″

A Karelian birch inlaid cigar case. The lid is decorated with an oval plaque of tortoiseshell and black enamel depicting the imperial crest.

5⅞″

Karelian birch was a popular material in Russia and also used for fine furniture in the eighteenth and nineteenth centuries.

Rectangular gold-mounted birchwood case decorated with two intertwined gold Vs on the lid. Cabochon sapphire thumbpiece.

3¼″

top to bottom:
A Russian Karelian birch case with a
two-color gold decorative mount on the
cover showing an arrow and laurel sprigs,
and centered with a round turquoise
stone. Match compartment and place for
tinder cord.
4⅜″. Inventory No. 15300

A birch case of rectangular oval section,
with a match compartment with striker
plate and a place for a tinder cord. Gold
thumbpiece set with a cabochon ruby.
4″

A birch case. The lid is decorated with an
enameled brass plaque with two birds.
3½″

Small wooden case. Moscow.
3⁷⁄₁₆″

clockwise from top:
Silver-mounted palisander case with yellow diamond thumbpiece.
Initials of MICHAEL PERCHIN, FABERGÉ in Cyrillic. 3⅞"

A palisander case with hollow gold interlacing initials applied on the lid, and a match compartment with striker plate and a tassel. Rose-cut diamond thumbpiece.
Initials of HENRIK WIGSTRÖM. St. Petersburg 1908–17. 3⅞". Inventory No. 16942

A two-color gold-mounted palisander case applied with gold sunburst decoration and two intertwining leaf vines and a cabochon sapphire thumbpiece. Match case and tindercord compartment at the ends.
Initials of MICHAEL PERCHIN, FABERGÉ in Cyrillic. St. Petersburg pre-1896. 3⅞". Inventory No. 1289. Exhibition: "Fabergé in America"

clockwise from top:

Gold-mounted tubular palisander case with a cabochon emerald thumbpiece. Initials of JOHANN VIKTOR AARNE, FABERGÉ in Cyrillic. St. Petersburg pre-1896. 3⅛″. Inventory No. 1250

A silver and wood case with cabochon sapphire thumbpiece. The silver decoration on lid is in the rococo style. KF in Cyrillic. 3¾″. Exhibition: "Carl Fabergé: Goldsmith to the Tsar"

Wooden case of oval section with two-color gold swags and ribbons decorated with the letter "B" in gold inside the wreath and set with rose-cut diamonds. Cabochon moonstone thumbpiece. Initials of HENRIK WIGSTRÖM, FABERGÉ in Cyrillic. St. Petersburg 1896–1908. 3¾″. Inventory No. 627 R

A wooden case. Its lid is decorated with a commemorative silver medal portraying Alexander I of Russia (1801–1825). Medal engraved inside: "ORBIS TE LAVDAT PACATVS MDCCCXIV." Silver-set small cabochon ruby thumbpiece. Initials of EDUARD SCHRAMM, FABERGÉ in Cyrillic. St. Petersburg 1908–17. 4⅜″

clockwise from top left:
A Russian wooden case. The lid is
inlaid with a crowned red and white
enamel military cross and an epaulette.
Cross has date 1835.
4⅜"

A Karelian birch case set with imperial
monograms. Its lid is decorated with a
gold Russian double-headed eagle, the
center of which is set with Cyrillic
letters in a circular pattern against
blue enamel and flanked by the digits
"1903" set with rose-cut diamonds.
Five other monograms in gold, one
beneath a crown.
6¼"

A presentation wooden case of oval
section. Its lid is decorated with a gold
Russian imperial crest.
4¾"

A large Karelian birch imperial presentation signature case. Its lid is applied
with numerous mementos in gold and
enamel, including the imperial yacht
and various imperial emblems.
5½"

top:
Silver-gilt tubular case with red enamel over waved *guilloché* ground. Rose-cut diamond thumbpiece. The case opens to reveal a striker plate on one side and a match compartment on the other.
Initials of HENRIK WIGSTRÖM, FABERGÉ, CF, London import marks. St. Petersburg 1908–17. 3¾″. Exhibitions: "Fabergé in America"; "Carl Fabergé: Goldsmith to the Tsar"

bottom:
Red enamel case with a green leather slipcase and cabochon moonstone in the corner.
Initials of ANDERS NEVALAINEN, KFABERGÉ in Cyrillic, imperial warrant. St. Petersburg 1896–1908. 3¾″. Inventory No. 9831

above, top to bottom:
A small silver-and-niello matchbox in
floral pattern with engraved initials.
2⅛″

An unusual and very rare silver-and-niello
case with floral design.
FABERGÉ in Cyrillic with imperial
warrant, import marks. Moscow 1896–1908. 4″.
Inventory No. 16924, 7036A
*This case is one of only a few silver-and-
niello cases known to exist.*

opposite:
Gilded silver mauve *guilloché* enamel over
sunburst pattern emanating from a rose-
cut diamond. Tan leather slipcase.
Initials of ANDERS NEVALAINEN, KFABERGÉ in Cyrillic,
imperial warrant. St. Petersburg 1896–1908. 3⅛″.
Inventory No. 6290

opposite:
Imperial presentation case of silver-gilt
oval section with translucent emerald
green enamel over moiré *guilloché*
ground. Decorated with chased two-
color gold palmette border; the hinged
lid is ornamented with a row of seed
pearls. Diamond thumbpiece. Original
fitted case. The case is inscribed:
"Nicky Alix 15 VI 1907."
Initials of HENRIK WIGSTRÖM. St. Petersburg
1896–1908. 4″. Exhibitions: "Fabergé in America";
"Carl Fabergé: Goldsmith to the Tsar"
*Presented by Czar Nicholas II and Czarina
Alexandra Feodorovna on the date that
Grand Duchess Maria Pavlovna and
Swedish Prince Wilhelm were engaged.
They married May 3, 1908. The cigarette
case must have been an engagement gift to
the groom or to his father, King Gustav V,
a heavy smoker.*

above:
Silver-gilt and emerald green *guilloché* enamel
vanity/cigarette case with three compartments
containing an ivory tablet, a mirror, and a
cabochon-sapphire–tipped pencil. The interior is
engraved with a princely crown and "S. Sch."
There are two cream-colored tassels. The four
thumbpieces are set with cabochon sapphires.
Initials of AUGUST HOLLMING, FABERGÉ in Cyrillic. St. Petersburg
1896–1908. 3½″. Inventory No. 16256. Exhibition: "Fabergé in
America"

right: Interior view

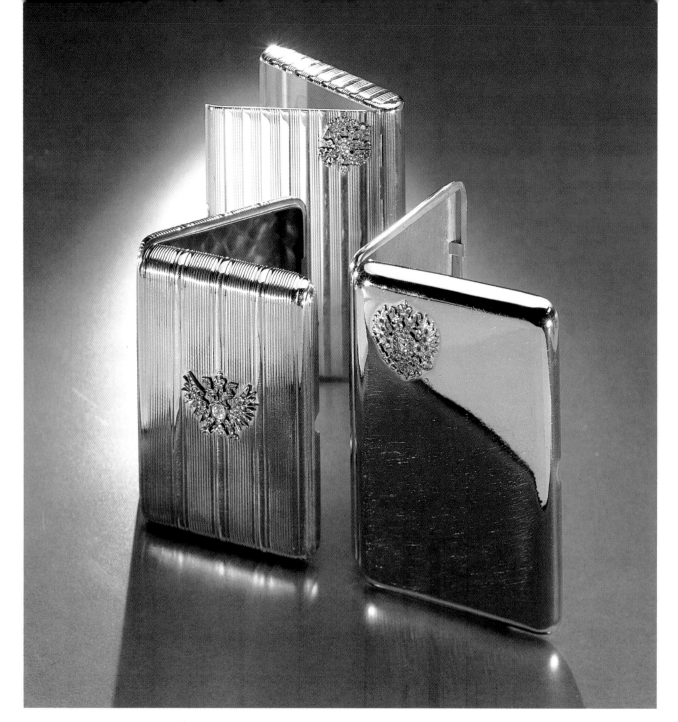

above, clockwise from top:
Gold imperial presentation case of reeded design with
alternating narrow stripes and polished wider stripes. The lid
is ornamented with a Russian imperial diamond-set gold
double-headed eagle in the corner, with rose-cut diamond
thumbpiece.
Initials of G. Lundell in Cyrillic. St. Petersburg 1896–1908. 3⅞″. Exhibition:
"Great Fabergé in the Hermitage"

An imperial gold presentation case. Its entire body is polished,
and one of the corners is set with a Russian double-headed
eagle set with rose-cut diamonds and rubies. Thumbpiece is
set with a cabochon sapphire.
KFabergé in Cyrillic, imperial warrant. Moscow 1908–17. 4″

Gold ribbed case, the cover applied with a diamond-set
Russian imperial eagle in the center. Cabochon sapphire
thumbpiece.
Initials of August Hollming, Fabergé in Cyrillic. St. Petersburg 1896–1908.
3½″

opposite, top to bottom:
A gold case whose entire body is decorated with engine-
turned bands alternating with polished double lines. The
sides are set with laurel-leaf bands. Thumbpiece with rose-cut
diamonds. Inscribed inside "In kind memory to dear
Gustav Ludwigovich from Bebut Khan 1-1-1917."
Initials of Henrik Wigström, Fabergé in Cyrillic. St. Petersburg 1908–17. 3⅞″

A two-color gold case. Its entire body is decorated with
alternating panels of reeded red gold and engine-turned
green gold further separated by opaque thin lines of white
champlevé enamel. The red-gold panels are further
ornamented with thin lines of royal blue champlevé enamel.
Thumbpiece set with a row of rose-cut diamonds.
Initials of Henrik Wigström, Fabergé in Cyrillic. St. Petersburg 1908–17. 3⅞″.
Inventory No. 25370. Exhibition: "Fabergé in America"

opposite:
Gold and translucent mauve enamel cigarette case. The
border of the cover is set all around with rose diamonds.
There are gold leaf borders at either end, and a single
pearl thumbpiece.

Initials of HENRIK WIGSTRÖM, FABERGÉ in Cyrillic. St. Petersburg,
1896–1908. 3⅞″. Inventory No. 522__

above:
Bright emerald green translucent enamel over moiré *guilloché* ground silver-gilt case, each end applied with two-
color gold palmette band. Concealed hinged match
compartment and diamond thumbpiece. In the original
wooden Fabergé case and stamped with the imperial warrant mark.

Initials of HENRIK WIGSTRÖM, CF, English import marks. St. Petersburg
1908–17. 3⅞″. Inventory No. 24594

Featured on the Fabergé Arts Foundation Christmas card, 1996.

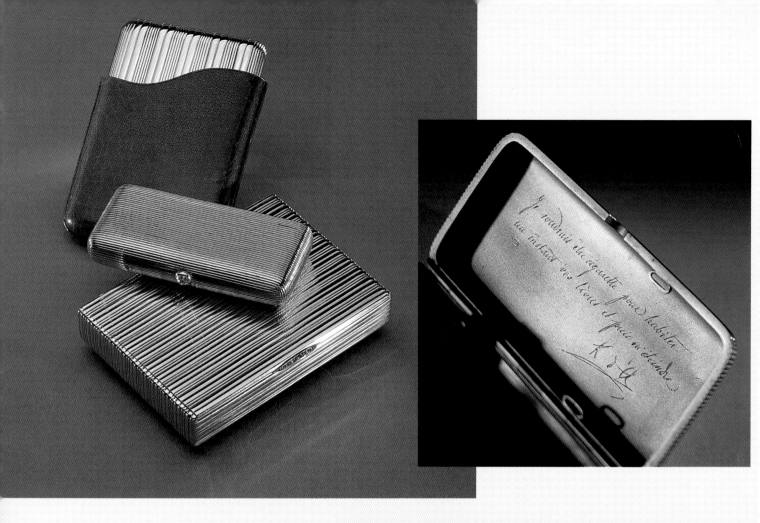

above, top to bottom:

Two-color gold open-ended case reeded with double bands of red gold and five narrow bands of green gold with spring hinge in leather slipcase.
Initials of August Hollming, Fabergé in Cyrillic, RL & Co., and import marks. St. Petersburg 1908–17. 3½". Inventory No. 17256 and 9752

A gold reeded lady's case with rounded corners and a diamond thumbpiece. Interior is engraved *"Je voudrais être une cigarette pour habiter un instant vos lèvres et puis m'éteindre"* ("I would like to be a cigarette, to live for an instant on your lips, and then go out").
Initials of Michael Perchin. St. Petersburg pre-1896. 3".
Exhibition: "Fabergé in America"

Rectangular gold case with alternating bands of narrow and wide stripes. Diamond-set thumbpiece.
Initials of Henrik Wigström, Fabergé in Cyrillic. St. Petersburg 1908–17. 3½"

above right: Interior detail

right:

A swirled three-color gold columnar cane handle case banded with acanthus-leaf motif and topped with a cabochon carnelian.
Initials of Michael Perchin. St. Petersburg pre-1896. 4"; stand is 1⅛". Inventory No. 46871 and 7013

above, top to bottom:
Royal-blue-enamel swag design case on silver
with gold trim. Rose diamond thumbpiece.
Initials of FEODOR AFANASSIEV, FABERGÉ in Cyrillic.
St. Petersburg 1908–17. 3½″. Inventory No. 23630

A gold-mounted silver-gilt and enamel case
decorated with blue enamel over moiré
guilloché ground bordered by chased two-color
gold palmette bands. London import marks for
1913. Diamond-set thumbpiece. Interior
inscribed "From Olaf 1912."
Initials of HENRIK WIGSTRÖM, FABERGÉ, CF, London marks.
St. Petersburg 1908–17. 4½″. Inventory No. 22440.
Exhibition: "Fabergé in America"
*The giver of this case was possibly Prince
Alexander of Denmark (later King Olaf V of
Norway).*

A vertical silver-gilt and lavender *guilloché*
enamel case with two bands set with rose-cut
diamonds. Center applied with diamond-set
flower. Thumbpiece decorated with faceted
diamond.
Initials of HENRIK WIGSTRÖM, FABERGÉ, London import
marks. 3⅞₆″. Inventory No. 22055

left:
Translucent lime-green-enamel and silver case
with gold trim decorated over engraved
guilloché ground. Cabochon ruby thumbpiece.
KFABERGÉ in Cyrillic, initials of AUGUST HOLLMING.
St. Petersburg 1896–1908. 3½″. Exhibitions: "Fabergé and
Finland"; "Fabergé: Loistavaa Kultasepäntaidetta"

clockwise from top:

Polished gold case with crowned two-color gold monogram studded with diamonds surmounted by Russian imperial crown. The reverse with two coats of arms surmounted by Russian imperial crown. Cabochon sapphire thumbpiece.

KF ᴀʙᴇʀɢᴇ́ in Cyrillic, imperial warrant. Moscow 1896–1908. 3⅞". Inventory No. 25678

A gold imperial presentation case, with a burnished exterior and an enamel-, gold-, and diamond-crowned cipher of Grand Duke Alexis Alexandrovich on *guilloché* ground. Separate match compartment, blue tinder cord, and moonstone thumbpiece. In the original fitted case.

Initials of Aᴜɢᴜsᴛ Hᴏʟʟᴍɪɴɢ, Fᴀʙᴇʀɢᴇ́. St. Petersburg 1896–1908. 3¹³⁄₁₆". Inventory No. 7443. Exhibition: "Fabergé in America"

Grand Duke Alexis, son of Czar Alexander II, and Admiral General and Supreme Chief of the Russian Imperial Fleet, visited the United States in 1872 at the invitation of President Ulysses S. Grant. He was the only member of the Russian imperial family ever to pay a state visit to the United States.

An imperial gilded silver presentation case, the lid applied with the enameled crowned cipher of Grand Duke Michael Michaelovich: two intertwined Ms on the cover—one red, one white—and blue on the crown. Back pierced with a compartment for a tinder cord. Match compartment. Reverse inscribed "Presented by H.I.H. the Grand Duke Michael of Russia. President Cannes Golf Club, won by Lt. Colonel CW Cragg, March 20, 1895."

Initials of Aᴜɢᴜsᴛ Hᴏʟᴍsᴛʀö̈ᴍ. St. Petersburg pre-1896. 3⅞"

Grand Duke Michael lived in Cannes for a number of years with his morganatic wife before moving to London.

clockwise from top:
A polished silver case of oval curved section applied with a gold monogram and enameled flags of imperial Russia and the United States. Cabochon ruby thumbpiece.
Initials of Anders Nevalainen, Fabergé in Cyrillic, imperial warrant. St. Petersburg 1896–1908. 3⅞″. Inventory No. 11835

A silver case with four triangles of alternating diagonal reeding. The center is set with an 1887 enamel miniature of St. George and the dragon contained within a beveled gold rim. Cabochon red stone thumbpiece is set in gold. Gilt interior, with a match compartment and striker plate.
Initials of Anders Nevalainen, KFabergé in Cyrillic. St. Petersburg 1896–1908. 4″

A silver case with wire-brushed surface and gilt interior. The lid is set with a Russian eighteenth-century silver coin decorated with red *guilloché* enamel. The coin is of the period of Elizabeth Petrovna. Cabochon sapphire thumbpiece.
Initials of Anders Nevalainen, KFabergé in Cyrillic, imperial warrant. St. Petersburg 1896–1908. 3½″. Inventory No. 5992

A silver case with fluted and wavy design. The lid is applied with an enameled life raft inscribed "San Toy." Pushing the front panel opens the case.
Initials of August Hollming, Fabergé in Cyrillic, English import marks. St. Petersburg 1908–17. 3⅜″

Oval enamel badge of the Moscow Automobile Society. The society's name is in Cyrillic and a red enamel center.
1½″
The Moscow Society was a chapter of the Imperial Russian Automobile Society, head-quartered in St. Petersburg on Dvortsovaya Naberezhnaya near the Winter Palace. The first president of the imperial society, which was founded in May 1903, was Count Frederichs, a friend and advisor of Nicholas II.

A silver-fluted swirl-design case. Its lid is decorated with a circular miniature with St. George slaying the dragon on red *guilloché* enamel ground within a gold rim. Match compartment and space for tinder cord. Cabochon red-stone thumbpiece.
Initials of Anders Nevalainen, KFabergé in Cyrillic, imperial warrant. St. Petersburg 1896–1908. 4¼″. Inventory No. 13726

center:
Silver commemorative Automobile Club cigarette case. The cover is decorated with bands of swags and urns; the center has a raised octagonal palmette motif enclosing the engraved emblem of the Moscow Automobile Club and the date 1911. Gilt interior with dedication inscription in Russian "Yeletz to Lipetzk, Yussa, driver P.A. Vedernikov, 1911." Thumbpiece of silver gilt.
KFabergé in Cyrillic, imperial warrant. Moscow 1908–17. 3⅜″. Inventory No. 25236. Exhibition: "Fabergé in America"

Jeweled gold-and-enamel case. The lid and base are enameled in translucent strawberry red over a lightly engine-turned ground overlaid with diamond-set trelliswork. The blue *taille d'epargne* enamel borders are decorated with carnations. Cabochon ruby thumbpiece.
Initials of KARL KARLOWITCH HAHN. St. Petersburg pre-1896. 3¾″
Featured on the Fabergé Arts Foundation Christmas card, 1996.

Magnificent gold-and-red-enamel tubular case swirled with gold stripes, and leaf borders at the ends. Diamond thumbpiece.
Initials of Michael Perchin, Fabergé in Cyrillic. St. Petersburg pre-1896. 3½″
Featured on the Fabergé Arts Foundation Christmas card, 1996.

clockwise from top:
Soldier's silver bowl or drinking cup (*charka*). This item is sometimes called an ashtray. Two rings around the edge, and the center is marked in Cyrillic "WAR 1914 KFABERGÉ."

KFABERGÉ in Cyrillic, imperial warrant. Moscow 1908–17. 4¼″

Brass soldier's bowl or drinking cup. This item is sometimes called an ashtray. Marked in Cyrillic "WAR 1914 KFABERGÉ."

KFABERGÉ in Cyrillic. 4⁵⁄₁₆″

A red copper case with a Russian imperial crest below the inscription "WAR 1914–1915."

KFABERGÉ in Cyrillic. 3½″. Exhibition: "Great Fabergé in the Hermitage"

Such cigarette cases in brass, copper, or silver were presented to soldiers and officers during World War I.

A silver war case with a repoussé double-headed eagle and "WAR 1914*1915," also inscribed above "KFABERGÉ 1916–1917."

KFABERGÉ, KF in Cyrillic, imperial warrant. Moscow 1908–17. 3¾″

War issue to an officer.

Silver World War I bowl engraved "WAR 1914 KFABERGÉ" in Cyrillic. Also sometimes referred to as an ashtray or soldier's drinking cup.

4½″

Such silver articles were reserved for the officers.

A silver case decorated with a repoussé Russian double-headed imperial eagle inscribed with "WAR 1914–1915" and "KFABERGÉ" in Cyrillic below. The reverse is inscribed "Carol Petrograd An 4 de la Guerre 1917."

KFABERGÉ in Cyrillic, imperial warrant. Moscow 1908–17. 3¾″

A gift to Countess Shakhanowskaya by King Carol of Romania.

A circular copper bowl (previously described as an ashtray), or soldier's drinking cup. In the bottom is the Romanoff double eagle and Russian inscription "WAR 1914–1915" and "KFABERGÉ" in Cyrillic.

KFABERGÉ in Cyrillic. 4½″

center:
Brass case decorated with a repoussé Russian double-headed imperial eagle with "WAR 1914–1917" and "KFABERGÉ" in Cyrillic below.

3¾″

clockwise from top:

A gold case decorated with an intertwined two-color gold monogram on one side and a gold anchor set with cabochon sapphires and old cut diamonds on the other side. Gilt interior. Cabochon sapphire thumbpiece.

JOSIF MARSHAK. Kiev 1908–17. 4⅛″

A silver presentation case. Its lid is decorated with a crowned anchor and a letter "K" studded with rose-cut diamonds and rubies. Cabochon ruby thumbpiece.

Initials of AUGUST HOLLMING, FABERGÉ in Cyrillic. St. Petersburg 1908–17. 3⅝″. Exhibition: "Fabergé in America"

The initial K is either for Grand Duke Kirill Vladimirovich (1876–1938), captain in the Russian imperial navy and commander of the cruiser Oleg, *or for Grand Duke Konstantin Konstantinovich (1858–1918), chief of the equipage of the navy.*

A large polished silver case. Its lid is decorated with a mast and three enameled flags. Match compartment and tassel. Interior inscription in Cyrillic "To Osip Osipovich In memory of the trip from Folero in the Crimea September 1899."

GAVRIL PETROVITCH GRACHEV. St. Petersburg pre-1896. 4⅜″

A large Russian silver repoussé case with an elephant amid tropical foliage. Cabochon sapphire thumbpiece.

Initials of CH in Cyrillic, unknown workmaster. Moscow 1908–17. 4½″

A Russian silver repoussé and engraved large case. Its lid is decorated with an elephant's head and stylized foliate design. The lid is also engraved with an inscription, "To Dear Company Commander Second Lieutenant S. P. Komarov-Lavrentyev, 2-28-1916." Back is also engraved in Russian. Gilt interior. Cabochon emerald thumbpiece.

Initials of ALEXANDER IVANOVICH PISKARYEV in Cyrillic. Moscow 1908–17. 4⅜″

A round silver bowl—sometimes referred to as an ashtray—more recently revealed as a soldier's drinking cup. The center is set with a Russian silver ruble coin with Catherine the Great, dated 1763. The exterior is decorated with a foliate border design and dates 1914–16.

Initials of ALEXANDER WÄKEVA, KFABERGÉ in Cyrillic, imperial warrant. St. Petersburg 1908–17. 4½″ Exhibition: "Fabergé and Finland"

A silver case of oval section, the lid repoussé with a ship on the sea. Match and tinder cord compartments. Gilt interior inscribed "For my dearest old man. God bless you xxx Halepa 1900."

Initials of MICHAEL PERCHIN, FABERGÉ in Cyrillic. St. Petersburg 1896–1908. 4″

left:
Case of light pink enamel over a *guilloché* ground of reeds and pellets. Of oval section. On one side is a princely crown. The lip has a diamond border, and the thumbpiece is diamond-set.
Initials of MICHAEL PERCHIN, FABERGÉ in Cyrillic. St. Petersburg 1896–1908. 3½″. Inventory No. 3561. Exhibition: "Fabergé in America"

right:
Case of oblong oval section of greenish-white translucent enamel on waved *guilloché* ground with chased gold acanthus-leaf bands. The monogram is in rose-cut diamonds below a royal crown applied on one side. Cabochon sapphire thumbpiece.
Initials of HENRIK WIGSTRÖM. St. Petersburg 1896–1908. 3¾″. Exhibition: "Fabergé in America"
Belonged to Prince Juan Fulco di Savoia, Spanish ambassador to Russia, 1887–91

A silver-and-red-enamel Soviet case, with rounded corners. The lid is decorated with repoussé hammer and sickle. Cabochon garnet thumbpiece. Initials of BXTM—an unknown post-revolutionary Soviet maker. Moscow 1908–17. 4½″

A polished silver case engraved with a globe within a wreath and further decorated with a red enameled star with a hammer and sickle underneath. Two inscribed interlaced initials below. Back engraved in Cyrillic. Red cabochon stone thumbpiece. Unknown Soviet maker. Moscow 1908–17. 4⅝″

A silver-and-red-enamel Soviet case. Its lid decorated in the Constructivist style, showing symbols of socialist industrialization. Cabochon green stone thumbpiece. Reverse side engraved in Cyrillic. M_ (partially rubbed out). Moscow 1908–17. 4⅝″

A Soviet silver case, the lid repoussé and engraved with a Red Army soldier clutching his rifle, with a large red star superimposed by a factory and a granary in the background. The case is executed in the Constructivist style. Engraved inside in Cyrillic "On Guard!" Cabochon sapphire thumbpiece. Unknown post-revolutionary Soviet maker. 1908–17. 3⅝″

A silver case. Its lid is engraved with an airplane whose wings bear red enameled stars. Below, a larger star and "CCCP" (USSR) in red enamel. Back is engraved "J Mac-Callum From the management and workers the E-L, L. Krassin for strong and quick job Baku 19 ²⁸XII 31 [December 28, 1931]." Cabochon sapphire thumbpiece. Initials of P.G. in Cyrillic—unknown Soviet maker. Moscow 1908–17. 4⅝″ *Included in case is the Protection Certificate and Certificate of Identity of James McCallum issued on January 28, 1919.*

An early Soviet silver and bright-red enameled case. Its lid is decorated with a Soviet flag inscribed "CCCP" above a red star superimposed with a hammer, sickle, and sheaf of wheat. Red cabochon stone thumbpiece. Unknown Soviet maker. Moscow 1908–17. 4¼″

clockwise from top:

A large elongated silver case with a gilt interior. The lid is repoussé with a half-naked female figure carrying arrows and embracing and leaning on a lion. Below is a Russian inscription reading "Power and Love."

Unknown Soviet maker, initials in Cyrillic. Moscow 1908–17. 4⅜"

Polished silver case ornamented on the lid with a repoussé polar bear and a sunset in the background. Cabochon citrine thumbpiece.

Unknown Soviet maker. Moscow 1908–17. 4⅛"

A silver Soviet case executed in the Constructivist style with a factory in the background, an aircraft in the sky, and a worker standing in the foreground holding his tools. Gilt interior, cabochon red-stone thumbpiece.

Unknown Soviet maker. Moscow 1908–17. 4⅜"

A silver case decorated with a battle scene. In the foreground a nurse attends to a wounded soldier sitting next to a cannon; in the background there is an attack by light cavalry. Thumbpiece is in silver.

Initials of AK. Kiev 1908–17. 4½"

Silver case in neo-Russian style. Its lid is decorated with a repoussé profile of a Russian boyar over a pan-Slavic ornament set with stones, the upper right corner with a gold maritime motif with rose-cut rubies and sapphires. Interior inscription dated January 29, 1906. Cabochon sapphire thumbpiece. In the original fitted box.

KFabergé in Cyrillic, imperial warrant. Moscow 1896–1908. 3½". Inventory No. 21133. Exhibition: "Fabergé in America"

A polished silver case engraved with a building of the Admiralty with an alley of trees in the front. Bottom inscribed "Leningrad, Admiralty."

Unknown Soviet maker. Moscow 1908–17. 4"

center:

A silver case. Its lid is repoussé with a worker forging steel, a factory billowing smoke from its chimneys in the background, and airplanes in the sky. Cabochon red stone thumbpiece.

Initials of P.G. in Cyrillic—unknown Soviet maker. Moscow 1908–17. 4⅜"

This scene is typical of Soviet Socialist workers' propaganda.

Silver-gilt and gold case with lavender *guilloché* enamel. Solid gold flower on either end, match compartment.
Initials of MICHAEL PERCHIN, FABERGÉ in Cyrillic. St. Petersburg pre-1896. 3⅞″. Inventory No. 1727

A silver-gilt and navy blue *guilloché* enamel case of rectangular section, the gold borders chased with laurel leaves. Match and tinder cord compartments, and diamond-set thumbpiece. The interior lid is engraved with a European coat of arms. In fitted Wartski case.

Initials of IVAN BRITZIN, London import marks. St. Petersburg 1908–17. 4¾″

Contains House of Commons brand original cigarettes and English coat of arms on inside cover.

clockwise from top:

Imperial silver and gold presentation case of oval section. The hinged cover is inlaid with a gold Cyrillic inscription "Christmas 1875." The reverse with similar gold name "Minny," nickname for Marie Feodorovna, wife of Alexander III. Tinder cord and match compartment with striker plate on outside.

Initials of SAMUEL ARNDT. St. Petersburg pre-1896. 4⅛″

Gift from Empress Marie Feodorovna to her future son-in-law, Grand Duke Alexander Mikhailovich on Christmas, 1875. Inherited by Prince Michel Romanoff de Russie from his father, Prince Theodor of Russia, son of the Grand Duke Alexander and Grand Duchess Xenia, sister to Czar Nicholas II.

Large silver case. The top of the lid is repoussé in high relief with two facing griffons separated by a rectangular area containing a two-color gold monogram with Cyrillic "TN" within a neo-Greek key border. Below are numerous engraved signatures. Cabochon sapphire set in gold thumbpiece.

KFABERGÉ in Cyrillic, imperial warrant. Moscow 1908–17. 4⅜″. Inventory No. 34635

A polished silver case with gilt interior and match compartment. The lid is set with a diagonal deep-blue champlevé enamel inscription in Russian, *"Golyuba,"* which translates to "My Dove" or "To My Dove," or "Darling."

KF and FABERGÉ in Cyrillic. St. Petersburg 1908–17. 3⅞″

The case is marked in a rather unorthodox way: It has a full signature of Fabergé right next to the initials KF. In most cases the firm's signature is followed by the workmaster's initials. Fabergé's initials and surname are to be found on the works of Nevalainen and Rappoport.

Polished silver case of rectangular oval section. The cover bears a blue enameled inscription (enamel worn), "Yrs. lovingly Sophy. Ventnor. 1891." With match and tinder compartments and concealed compartment inside the hinged cover fitted for an oval miniature photograph. Gilt interior and cabochon ruby thumbpiece.

Initials of AUGUST HOLMSTRÖM. St. Petersburg pre-1896. 3⅜″

Sophy de Torby married Grand Duke Michael Michaelovich and was the mother of Nada, who married George Mountbatten, 2nd Marquess of Milford Haven.

clockwise from top:

A polished silver case in the Russian revival style. Its lid is decorated with repoussé design, in pan-Slavic motif encircling a matte-finished enameled miniature painting of a young maiden with a baby goat.
Initials of WILHELM REIMER, FABERGÉ in Cyrillic. St. Petersburg 1908–17. 4⅜″. Exhibition: "Great Fabergé in the Hermitage"
The miniature painting refers to the Russian tale "Little Sister Alyonushka and Little Brother Ivanushka," in which Ivan turns into a goat after drinking the water his sister warned him not to drink.

Silver open-work over matte enamel case chased and repoussé with a rearing bear attacking a man in the traditional Old Russian medieval boyar costume. Trees in the background and a painted enamel winter landscape underneath. Cabochon emerald thumbpiece.
Initials of FEODOR RÜCKERT, KFABERGÉ in Cyrillic. Moscow 1908–17. 4⅜″
Exhibition: "Great Fabergé in the Hermitage"

Silver case repoussé and chased with three legendary heroes from Russian history after a painting by Yuri Alekseevich Vasnetsov. Silver-set cabochon orange stone thumbpiece.
1908–17. 4⅛″
The painting by Vasnetsov is called The Bogatyrs *and was reproduced on many decorative objects at the turn of the century. It is a very large painting now in the Tretyakov Gallery in Moscow.*

Oval section, two-color gold-mounted salmon-pink enamel case over swag design. Raised laurel-leaf trim on either end. Diamond thumbpiece.

Initials of HENRIK WIGSTRÖM, FABERGÉ in Cyrillic. St. Petersburg 1908–17. 3⅛″. Exhibition: "Carl Fabergé: Goldsmith to the Tsar"

Commentaries

FTER an eighty-year hiatus, Fabergé history has become new history. The opening of the Soviet archives has released a flood of information that is helping to shed new light on this previously inaccessible cache of art treasures.

The esteemed historians and consultants in this section have pursued this trail of material on Fabergé's workmasters, designers, and craftsmen, formulating new insights about Carl Fabergé and his relationships with the czars and his contemporaries, and unraveling old mysteries surrounding his work. Some pieces have not been seen since the 1917 revolution, while others have only recently been discovered. More is being learned every day.

Those historians and followers of Russian art with particular insight into Fabergé cigarette cases share their distinctive knowledge here.

GALINA G. SMORODINOVA
Scientific Researcher, State Historical Museum, Moscow
(translated by Andre Ruzhnikov)

THE HISTORY of tobacco is measured in centuries and is full of legends, dramas, tragedies, and adventures. Tobacco has been forbidden, and it has also been smoked as a symbol of peace and armistice. It has been considered to have some positive medical uses in some years, and it has been thought to be a great foe of health in others. We are in the foe-of-health stage right now.

Tobacco was brought to Russia by the English in 1553, unloaded from a ship in the city of Arkhangelsk along with salt, wine, and paper. Though not practiced by the government of Czar Ivan the Terrible, by the first part of the seventeenth century tobacco use had become widespread. Even the clergy of Russia—the keepers of morality—couldn't keep it in check. When Czar Mikhail became the Russian ruler in 1613, the church demanded severe punishment of smokers; they were tortured and whipped, and those who had multiple violations had their noses cut off.

Superstitions came to life, some of them claiming that tobacco was the devil's plant and was used to communicate with evil forces. There was a belief that it conquered people's souls. Tobacco was considered sinful. Some said that weeds, including tobacco or something else that could be sniffed or smoked, grew only on bad people's graves. Good people's graves were covered with roses and lilies and other beautiful plants.

When Peter the Great reigned (1689–1725), the ideas changed, and Peter took up smoking himself. To introduce it to his countrymen, he concluded a contract with Englishman Lord Karmaten, giving him the right to sell tobacco across the entire country of Russia. Though the contract stipulated a fee of £200,000, Lord Karmaten only gave £12,000 to Peter. The Englishman started making so much money that after seven years the agreement was rescinded. It had become apparent that the Russian use of tobacco was a growing trend; it was getting to be a big business. Foreigners had to move aside. In 1714 the first Russian tobacco-processing factory was opened. Smoking and sniffing had become fashionable.

The tobacco industry was supported by the government through loans and free seeds. Russian tobacconists were sent abroad to study, and in 1763 an office dealing with supplying Russian tobacco farmers with American seeds was created. In 1768 a French gentleman named Bouchet was given 16,000 rubles to open a cigarette-processing factory in St. Petersburg, along with a school for tobacconists. In 1838 there were 120 tobacco-processing factories, both large and small, and by 1860 the number had grown to 551. The best-known factories in St. Petersburg were Shaposhnikov, Saatchi, Mangubi, and Miller, and in Moscow there were Ducat, Popov, and Reinguard.

In museum archives one can find original boxed cigarettes of the time. They were very colorful, and advertising was ingenious—full of humor and responding to the mood of society. A church in the Winter Palace in St. Petersburg had a special staircase where the Grand Dukes could smoke because it was not permitted to smoke in church during the service.

Cigarette cases can be seen as historical monuments. They reflect Russian culture and important historical events; they illuminate the views of different cities and the lives of different strata of society. It is a well-known fact that the St. Petersburg and Moscow styles of the time were different, catering to the tastes of European or Russian clientele. The St. Petersburgers preferred the styles of Fabergé, Bolin, Morozov, Britzin, and Grachev Brothers, while the Muscovites fancied those of Ovchinnikov and Khlebnikov and the Fabergé Moscow workshops.

The cases were repoussé, engraved, cast, enameled, and applied with Russian proverbs and wisecracks. Just looking at cigarette cases, one could pick up the peculiarities of a certain individual; likewise, one could judge a person by looking at his or her cigarette case. It was particularly pleasant to pull out a cigarette case that matched one's attire. A person's social standing and romantic and family relationships could be gleaned from a case. Cigarette cases were a piece of everybody's life. In the second part of the nineteenth century, the entire populace of Russia smoked, from the Emperor down to the peasants.

For the coronation of Nicholas II in 1894, over 150 cigarette cases were produced and the Fabergé firm was awarded an order of St. Stanislaus Second Class. Captain Sablin, of the *Standard*, the imperial yacht, wrote, "Nicholas II has a wonderful collection of cigarette cases—one better than the other. And every day he uses a different one." When Nicholas used the yacht, all the cigarette cases were placed on a special table in his study, from which he could choose the one for the day.

One can easily imagine how these trinkets were treasured by their recipients.

DR. MARINA N. LOPATO
Curator of Western Applied Art
The State Hermitage Museum, St. Petersburg
(translated by Andre Ruzhnikov)

UNDER PETER THE GREAT the use of tobacco became widespread, particularly in the upper crust of society. In eighteenth-century Russia and Europe, it had become the "age of the snuffbox." Russian authors of the time, including Herzen, Pushkin, and Sollogub, often refer to the use of tobacco, in many cases emphasizing the materials from which the cigarette case was made—for instance, silver—thus underlining the social status of the owner.

The habit of using snuff (powdered tobacco) originated in the eighteenth century and was quite popular among women; men used snuff and smoked pipes. (After the war with Napoleon [1812–13] they also started smoking cigars.) In the nineteenth century the combination of pipes and cigars gave way to cigarettes, which were more democratic and less expensive. They were like the filterless cigarettes we know today; they were rolled by the smoker himself. A snuffbox and a little piece of paper were always available.

In the mid-nineteenth century, author Vladimir Dal explains that cigarettes were small cigars, or "papirosa." Papirosa were paper "pipes" filled with tobacco. The word came from the Egyptian word *papyrus.* Papirosas were used by men at least from the middle of the nineteenth century. In one story, French writer T. T. Gotier also mentions how common papirosa and cigars were at the time. Additionally, he emphasized that it was forbidden to smoke in the streets. In the same story he refers to watching a Gypsy chorus. During the performance, the Gypsy sits on the lap of members of the audience, passes her cigarette to the person's mouth, and then takes it back. Gypsies started smoking earlier than high-society ladies, who, in the late nineteenth century, smoked rather elongated ladies' cigarettes called *pakhitoska.* The origin of this word is not quite clear.

Gradually, as cigarettes became more and more widespread, they were equipped with paper extensions that eliminated the need for cigarette holders made out of amber, silver, or wood. This paper extension, which prevented smokers' fingers from being covered with yellowish tobacco residue, produced no tobacco aftertaste, unlike the rolled-up, cheaper variety peasants used.

To store cigarettes, cigarette cases and paper holders were designed. Paper holders were usually cylindrical and placed on top of the box. Cigarette cases were in common use. These were flat boxes where cigarettes and papirosa were placed in one or two layers. In the event that there was enough room for two layers, either side had elastic bands to keep the contents in place. Cigarette cases were ordinarily situated on tables and were often equipped with some automatic device that enabled a cigarette to jump out from the box, usually belonging to well-to-do people.

Going through the archival materials of the Cabinet of His Imperial Majesty, one continuously finds invoices from jewelers, including Fabergé, presented to the Court. Though the Fabergé invoices covered a variety of items starting in the 1880s, cigarette cases predominated. When Fabergé became the purveyor to the imperial Court, only a few cigarette cases were ordered. But by the beginning of the twentieth century, the number of cases was calculated in several dozens. In the 1890s there had been many more snuffboxes made, but at the start of this century, they had given way to cigarette cases, most of which were purchased by the imperial Cabinet from Fabergé for presentation, given on behalf of the Emperor or Empress.

One of the first cigarette cases purchased from Fabergé, in 1885, for the imperial Cabinet was made with sapphires, numbered 31604, and priced at 252 rubles. The piece was presented to an unknown person during the imperial visit to Copenhagen. There was another silver cigarette case with a gold coat of arms, that cost 75 rubles. During later years, standard silver cigarette cases with a gold coat of arms cost between 72 and 80 rubles. In the event that rose-cut diamonds were added to the coat of arms, the price rose to 125 rubles. In 1891 the heir apparent, Nicholas II, took a trip to the Far East. The imperial Cabinet ordered quite a few things from Fabergé, among them silver cigarette cases with gold eagles and sapphires, with inventory numbers 692–887. Silver cigarette cases with gold eagles only were inventoried 437–448 and were priced at 45 to 80 rubles.

The years 1892 and 1893 saw the Emperor and Empress traveling extensively and hence there were large orders from Fabergé, including a gunmetal case, an onyx case, and three silver ones. On February 5, 1893, the imperial Cabinet paid 100 rubles for a cigarette case made of white leather. As a result of the death of Alexander III and transfer of his body, three cigarette cases were listed as items purchased by the imperial Cabinet. Two of them were with diamonds and pearls, ranging in price from 445 to 575 rubles.

On the occasion of their wedding, Grand Duchess Xenia Alexandrova and Grand Duke Alexander Mikhailovich received from the imperial family (among other precious things) a gold cigarette case in the Louis XV style, embellished with rose-cut diamonds, priced at 800 rubles. Two gold cigarette cases, numbered 50892 and 41761, were shipped to Copenhagen in conjunction with the visit of Empress Marie Feodorovna. A cigarette case with white enamel and green stripes and another of steely colored enamel appear in the list of acquisitions. During the Czar's 1900 short trip, two cigarette cases, numbered 610 and 6219, were presented.

The largest orders from the imperial Court were made in 1895–96, in conjunction with the coronation of Nicholas II. The archival materials containing the invoices and orders are extensive. They consist of six large parts and are filled with invoices of various purveyors of jewelry and silver items. Fabergé invoices are dated 5/17/96, 6/9, 6/14, 6/17, and 7/19 and list forty-four cigarette cases—among them cheap silver with double-headed eagles for 100 to 175 rubles and others with diamonds and enamel, which ranged in price from 500 to 700 rubles. Then there was one of polished gold for 285 rubles, nephrite for 215 rubles, and so on.

And then again the imperial couple went on the road to Moscow, Livadia, Denmark, the Caucasus, and Nizhni Novgorod. As they went along, all sorts of objects, including cigarette cases, were given away on their behalf. It seems that when preparing for a trip inside Russia, the imperial Cabinet ordered more cigarette cases than it did when preparing for a trip abroad. Who were these presents intended for? Alas, the documents rarely point to the recipients of the Czar's gifts. Clerks only very infrequently wrote down the name of the happy recipients because they were not required to get receipts.

The simple silver cigarette cases were often given to the people servicing the Czar's cortege, Czar's train, railroad, security services, and so on. The recipients included bakers, police officers, coachmen, and people responsible for the train stations. More important people were given more expensive cigarette cases. For instance, when the ruler from Bukhara came to St. Petersburg, he was given a nephrite cigarette case with the cipher of His Imperial Majesty embellished with stones, priced at 1,350 rubles. Grand

Duke Mikhailovich presented a gold cigarette case, priced at 630 rubles, to the Governor General of Korea, Count Teraucci, during his trip to Japan.

There was an enormous number of orders given to Fabergé in 1913 in connection with the celebration of the jubilee of the Romanoff dynasty. Among the invoices that we managed to find, there were 156 imperial presentation cases. Someone received a precious case with blue enamel and precious stone (Fabergé inventory #4304). Steel cases were valued highly, from 360 to 800 rubles (#4305–4310). It is quite clear that the number of cigarette cases were growing, becoming standard items ordered by the imperial Cabinet. Many cases were kept in reserve for presents for people of different rank and service.

Cigarette cases were just a small part of Fabergé's business, but one can see every facet, every detail of his creativity through these small masterpieces. Fabergé produced items for members of different strata of society, starting from plain 15-ruble cigarette cases to resplendent pieces for the nobility for 800 rubles. I have had the chance to go through archives pertaining only to the imperial Court. There are innumerable other Fabergé cases ordered by people of lesser stature. I'd like to point out that as a rule, the inventory numbers mentioned in the invoices coincide with the inventory numbers scratched inside the cigarette cases. This might help the current owners of these cigarette cases to verify the dating and maybe even to discover the occasion for which the case was produced.

Joyce Lasky Reed
President, Fabergé Arts Foundation

DURING MY EARLY DAYS learning about Fabergé, I asked the noted expert Kenneth Snowman whether he owned any such objects. "Of course," he said, "I carry a Fabergé cigarette case with me all the time."

He pulled an enamel cigarette case from his breast pocket. It was rather plain, a beige-and-brown herringbone pattern. He opened the case, revealing a few cigarettes "just for show," then closed it and put it back in his jacket pocket.

I murmured something appropriate about it being lovely and how charming it was to carry Fabergé casually, as one would a handkerchief.

After a moment or two, I recalled his closing the case and realized something was missing. "But Kenneth," I said, "when you just shut the case, it made no clicking sound."

A broad smile lit up his face. "It makes no sound," he said. "That is the quality of the workmanship." He withdrew the case again, opened and closed it. Again, there was no click. The absence of a closing noise had a charm all its own.

"That, my dear, is Fabergé."

It was my first and most vivid lesson in Fabergé's genius.

MARILYN PFEIFER SWEZEY

Art historian and curator, Fabergé Arts Foundation

NICHOLAS II presented hundreds of cigarette cases decorated with the Russian imperial eagle or an imperial monogram to his uncles, as well as the Grand Dukes, cousins, foreign relatives, diplomats, Russian officials, and various people who had served him or the country in a special way. The white enameled cigarette case with the crowned cipher in gold of Grand Duke Nicholas Nicholaevich (cousin of Nicholas II and Russian military commander of 1914–15) is characteristic of these gifts and a wonderful example of the simple elegance of the Fabergé style (see p. 56).

Many of the cigarette cases are decorated primarily in the transparent colored enameling that was the special achievement of the Fabergé workshops. Here can be found an open field of vibrant color, which changes in hue as the handheld case is moved about in different grades of light. The depth of glossy color over graceful patterns of *guilloché* work engraved on the metal underneath is a tangible delight to both the smoker and non-smoker. The powder-blue cigarette case with its pale ruby thumbpiece holds is similar in color to the Blue Drawing Room, where the great Fabergé exhibition at the Hermitage took place. This is a wonderful example of Fabergé enameling (see p. 55).

The Fabergé cigarette cases represent a wide range of styles, from neoclassical and rococo to Art Nouveau and *style moderne*. There is also an interesting variety of materials, from gold and silver with enameling to wood and copper, as can be seen in the cigarette case of red copper with the imperial eagle and inscription in Russian, "War 1914–1915 K. Fabergé" (see p. 148).

On January 23, 1915, the enameled cigarette case of deep cobalt blue set with the Russian imperial eagle in diamonds was presented to Prince N. A. Kudashev, an official of the Hermitage, on the highest order of the imperial Court, as the inscription inside the lid indicates (see p. 93).

Sometimes a Fabergé cigarette case was presented as a trophy to the winner of a competitive sporting event. The simple polished gold cigarette case with the crowned cipher of Grand Duke Michael Michaelovich in red and white enameling is such an example (see p. 144). The inscription on the reverse of the case in English tells us that it was "Presented by HIH The Grand Duke Michael of Russia President Cannes Golf Club" and that it was won by "Lt. Col. C. W. Cragg on March 20, 1895." Grand Duke Michael was obliged to leave Russia in 1891 when he married morganatically in Europe. His wife was given the title Countess Torby and for many years the couple lived very well in Cannes. Later they moved to London where one of their daughters, Zia, married Sir Harold Wernher.

Of special historical interest in the Traina Collection is the silver-gilt cigarette case in Art Nouveau style with an American connection (see p. 124). Decorated with repoussé poppies dotted with tiny cabochon sapphires and a faceted diamond, it bears an interior inscription in English: "Edward G. Pease Dayton, Ohio U.S.A." An accompanying note explains that this box was presented by Nicholas II to Edward Pease in appreciation for special iron construction work in Russia. It was later sold by his descendant Judge Pease, who had inherited it.

Two cigarette cases in the Traina Collection are particularly unusual in style (see p. 157). Made of silver and decorated with Russian-revival motifs in the Art Nouveau style, each one bears a painted enamel Russian scene with matte finish in the technique developed by independent Moscow workmaster Feodor Ruckert around 1908. One of these is a rare example of Ruckert's enameled pieces in the Russian-revival style, which were frequently sold through Fabergé. Seen through an openwork scene of a Russian boyar hunter attacked by a bear in a forest represented in repoussé silver samorodok is a picture of the Russian winter in painted enamel. The other is a rare example of a piece in the Russian-revival style made in St. Petersburg by workmaster W. R., possibly Wilhelm Reimer. The cigarette case of silver with Russian-revival motifs in repoussé is decorated with a charming enameled miniature painting of a maiden with a young goat, illustrating the popular Russian tale "Little Sister Alyonushka and Little Brother Ivanushka," in which Ivanushka turns into a goat after disobeying his sister's admonition not to drink water from a certain spring.

ALICE MILICA ILICH
Fabergé and Russian Art Consultant

IMAGINE a well-groomed gentleman nonchalantly reaching into his tailored jacket and bringing forth a simple and elegant gold-ribbed case, opening it with a single, graceful movement, and removing a cigarette. He taps it several times on the now-closed cover of his case before lighting its tip.

This image is easily evoked when holding one of the exquisitely crafted cigarette cases that formed the greater part of Fabergé's—and indeed his competitors'—stock during the Belle Époque.

In this era many Russian aristocrats traveled regularly to Paris for the social season, bringing with them their Russian accessories. Among them, and much admired, were their stunning cigarette cases set with their cipher or regimental insignia. Or they would sport a cigarette case that was adorned with a multitude of symbols, such as a champagne bottle, musical notes, a lady's slipper, or a line of verse, reminders of a night spent in unforgettable revelry or passionate love (see pp. 79–84).

An accessory such as the cigarette case or walking stick was a gentleman's means of displaying publicly his taste and social status. An awareness of style created a desire for more harmonious links between fashion and functional accessories. In the domain of cigarette cases, the Russian firm of Fabergé was a trendsetter even in the competitive fashion capital of Paris.

It was the craftsmanship of these cases, with their seamless hinges and concealed match and tinder-cord compartments that made them an indispensable part of the gentleman's wardrobe and earned him the admiration of his peers.

Fabergé's preoccupation with the detail and quality of a finished article meant that items were made by a series of craftsmen who were experts in specific areas, such as hinges or jeweled clasps. As a result, the completed articles were less the product of any one artist's creative inspiration than a technical tour de force.

top to bottom:
A large silver cigar case by Fabergé. Its lid is decorated with four Romanesque laurel wreaths and ribbons in the corners, four rosettes, and ribbon-tied octagon in the center. Gold thumbpiece set with a cabochon sapphire. Hole for tinder cord and match compartment.
KFABERGÉ in Cyrillic, imperial warrant. Moscow 1896–1908. 6¼". Exhibition: "Great Fabergé in the Hermitage"

Silver case applied with a chased key-pattern motif. The cover is applied with an octagonal cartouche enclosing the cast and chased figures of Hermes and Apollo, below which is an applied chased gold imperial eagle. Gold-mounted cabochon sapphire thumbpiece. Fitted case.
KFABERGÉ in Cyrillic, imperial warrant. Moscow 1908–17. 3¾". Inventory No. 26490

A silver fluted case, its lid set with a gold cipher "NN." Gold thumbpiece decorated with a cabochon ruby.
Initials of A. NEVALAINEN, KFABERGÉ in Cyrillic, RL & Co., import marks, imperial warrant. St. Petersburg 1896–1908. 3⁷⁄₁₆". Inventory No. 14887. Exhibition: "Great Fabergé in the Hermitage"
From the collection of S. Bulgari, Rome.

A Collection of
Collections: Museums

ERE, representatives of major American collections of Fabergé, as well as some from Russia, Sweden, and England, give their perspectives on their Fabergé holdings. Like all others, these collections started with the acquisition of that one first piece (often a cigarette case) and then blossomed into something much bigger. Many collectors have generously shared their proud possessions with the public, their collections traveling a circuit to distant venues to be enjoyed by an even wider audience, by those who are fascinated at a distance by the glamorous world of collecting.

Many other fine Fabergé collections exist, such as the one inherited by Lady Zia (daughter of Grand Duke Michael), at one time exhibited in her English country home, Luton Hoo, as well as the Hoover Institution's young and growing collection of Russian art, including Fabergé, in Stanford, California. The existing relatives of the last Czar and Czarina, along with Swiss, Crimean, German, and other American collectors, also have Fabergé collections.

I asked Fabergé collectors and those who appreciate and act as guardians to the remaining treasures from a bygone era to share some of their thoughts.

CHRISTOPHER FORBES
The FORBES Magazine Collection

EVERY COLLECTION begins with a first purchase which sparks the desire for more. For my father, Malcolm S. Forbes, it was a cigarette case by Peter Carl Fabergé that ignited an enthusiasm that has continued into the next generation. Wishing to buy my mother something special for Christmas in 1960, Pop presented her with a handsome gold cigarette case by Fabergé decorated with a diamond-studded double-headed eagle, symbol of the Romanoff dynasty. He was always proud of this first acquisition in spite of one scholar's dismissing it as "the kind of thing the Czar gave to stationmasters on state visits!"

This was the first of many cigarette cases and presentation boxes, as well as other smoking paraphernalia, to enter our Fabergé treasury. This first personal purchase eventually led to the establishment of a corporate collection. (It had also not escaped Pop's notice that FORBES Magazine was launched by his father, B. C. Forbes, in September 1917, one month prior to Lenin's ascension to power in Russia.)

Today, with both my mother and father gone, the cigarette case has joined the thousands of objets d'art in The FORBES Magazine Collection, which features a spectacular Fabergé ensemble. Each year approximately 65,000 visitors pass through the galleries, and we hope that Pop's love of Fabergé and collecting has been contagious to all.

JOHN WEBSTER KEEFE
Principal Curator of The Decorative Arts
New Orleans Museum of Art
Matilda Geddings Gray Foundation Collection

THE EIGHT splendid Fabergé cigarette cases in the Matilda Geddings Gray Foundation Collection cover a spectrum of style and technique. Their styles range from subtle historicism to opulent imperial Russian to austere modernism: technically, gold- and silversmithing, *guilloché* and champlevé enameling, and the lapidary arts are represented. These stylistic and technical depths reveal the genius of Fabergé's creativity. He was a master of both traditional and contemporary style, consistently achieving a dazzling union of design and technique. Through his consummate artistry, the relatively small, utilitarian cigarette case transcended function to become a visually arresting work of art.

ANNE ODOM
Chief Curator, Hillwood Museum
Marjorie Merriweather Post Collection

*T*HE FABERGÉ COLLECTION of Marjorie Merriweather Post (1887–1973), only a small part of a much larger collection of French and Russian decorative art, numbers almost ninety objects. In 1926 she bought her first piece of Fabergé, an amethyst quartz box with a lid fashioned from a piece of Mogul jewelry, from the collection of Prince Felix Iusupov.

In January 1937, Mrs. Post went to Moscow with her third husband, Joseph E. Davies, the newly appointed ambassador to the Soviet Union. During this tour she became fascinated with Russian art, an interest she was to sustain through the rest of her life. During their almost twenty years of marriage, Davies gave her many gifts of Fabergé. She acquired Fabergé pieces steadily through the 1950s and made a proportionately large number of purchases in the 1960s, when Marvin Ross, her curator, was writing his catalogue, *Fabergé and His Contemporaries*.

There are no cigarette cases by Fabergé in the collection, although there are several by other masters.

HARRY S. PARKER III
Director, Fine Arts Museums of San Francisco

*I*N 1954 The Fine Arts Museums of San Francisco received our first example of the work of Peter Carl Fabergé, a silver tea service and the table designed for it. This gift from our founder, Alma Spreckles, has been followed by other examples of Fabergé; the most recent were gifts from John Traina.

San Francisco has had a significant Russian population since shortly after the 1917 revolution, and when in 1964 the de Young Museum mounted an exhibition of Fabergé material, many of the loans came from local Russian collectors, several of whom were related to the imperial family.

Thirty years later, in developing the exhibition "Fabergé in America," we decided to focus upon the Americans, rather than the European aristocracy, who had collected Fabergé. In this connection, a group of thirty-three objects, primarily cigarette cases, was chosen from the collection of John Traina, a generous lender indeed. The smooth surfaces of the cases—which are made from a variety of materials—provide the perfect vehicle for the display of Fabergé's matchless enameling technique and exceptional palette.

"Fabergé in America" has toured the United States, where it was seen at five venues by thousands of visitors eager to experience the seductive design of this virtuoso designer.

LEE HUNT MILLER
Curator, European Decorative Arts and Sculpture,
Fine Arts Museums of San Francisco

IN THESE TIMES of antismoking regulations, one is apt to forget that during Peter Carl Fabergé's heyday, it was not only acceptable, but de rigueur to smoke cigarettes. Czar Nicholas was a great smoker, owning and giving as gifts many cigarette cases. We know that he kept a supply of these articles in the palace, ready to be given as commemorative presents to appropriate visitors, or as acknowledgments of kindnesses done to the monarch.

Members of the Court, both men and women, followed suit, and some of the cases were indeed extravagant in their materials and surface decoration. Many retained the silken tassel that was an anachronistic reminder that before the convenience of sulfur matches one had to use tinder and a stone to create the flame to light one's tobacco.

ELSEBETH WELANDER-BERGGREN
Guest curator, Nationalmuseum, Sweden

AMONG all the superb cigarette cases in John Traina's collection there is one that is connected to the Swedish royal family (see p. 137). The emerald green case is enameled over a moiré *guilloché* pattern. This moiré pattern is made in a very special way, typical of the work of one of Carl Fabergé's workmasters, Henrik Wigström. (Several of Fabergé's other workmasters—including Michael Perchin and Johan Viktor Aarne—of course used moiré *guilloché* patterns but in a quite different way.)

The case has the inscription "Nicky Alix 15.VI, 1907." The date is the day the Swedish Prince Wilhelm was engaged to Grand Duchess Maria Pavlovna. They married on May 3, 1908. The cigarette case must have been a gift from the Czar and Czarina for either the father of Prince Wilhelm, King Gustav V, who was a heavy smoker, or the groom himself.

HENRY HAWLEY
Chief Curator, Later Western Art, The Cleveland Museum of Art
India Early Minshall Collection
(excerpted from Géza von Habsburg, *Fabergé in America*)

MINSHALL . . . bought her first Fabergé piece in 1937, for $250, a charming little clock made of rhodonite with an enamel face inscribed "Fabergé" and surrounded by tiny diamonds. . . . She said, for example, that when presented with the choice of European travel or a Fabergé object, she customarily opted for the latter, despite the fact that exploring new places was a great pleasure for her. . . . Fabergé came to dominate her collecting activities in later life. If the Fabergé objects also had associations with the Romanovs, so much the better, but that was no longer a necessity.

Though not of enormous size, Minshall's Fabergé collection includes representative examples of every significant variety of object that Fabergé made. It is the remarkable degree of concurrence of historic importance, technical quality, and beauty of the particular pieces that makes this Fabergé collection a distinguished one.

The Royal Collection
The Queen's Gallery, Buckingham Palace
(excerpted from *Fabergé**)

FABERGÉ'S business was based on the premiss that the eggs, boxes, flowers, animals, birds and *bibelots* were to be given away as presents. They were not conceived as collectors' items which would be jealously guarded for private enjoyment by a fanatical collector in the mould of Balzac's 'Le cousin Pons'. Their primary role was to give pleasure, a pleasure shared in equal measure by both the recipient of the gift and the donor.

The collection formed by Queen Alexandra was characterized by a lack of ostentation, by restraint. Significantly, she did not own any of the more flamboyant pieces such as Easter Eggs. . . . Successive sovereigns have also left their mark on the collection. Mindful of the interest which men might take in his wares, Fabergé developed lines which had a more masculine appeal. Cigarette cases, lighters and match boxes are obvious examples. King Edward VII was one of the most fervent admirers of Fabergé. In addition to taking a personal interest in the development of Queen Alexandra's collection—he was constantly warning Bainbridge against supplying duplicates—he was not averse to receiving presents himself.

The enthusiasm of the British Royal Family for Fabergé has never waned. In Carl Fabergé's lifetime, the opening of the London shop was evidence of the importance he attached to the development of this connection.

---

* *Fabergé*, 1995. Catalogue, The Queen's Gallery, Buckingham Palace © 1995 The Royal Collection.

DR. DAVID PARK CURRY
Curator of American Arts
Virginia Museum of Fine Arts

*D*URING the late nineteenth century, long before the upper classes in other Western countries, Russian aristocrats embraced cigarette culture. Using their own blend of Turkish and Russian tobacco, noblemen—usually officers in elite regiments—smoked at Court. Women did not smoke in public; yet, as the numerous ladies' cases by Fabergé testify, the practice was socially acceptable in private.

While Lillian Thomas Pratt's first interest was in imperial Easter eggs (of which she owned five) and objects with intimate connections to the imperial family, she too was mesmerized by the beauty of cigarette cases. The pieces in her collection, generously given by bequest to the Virginia Museum of Fine Arts in 1947, are unique—as is each piece in the Traina Collection. Even when creating luxurious objects for everyday use on a common theme, the Fabergé workshops seem to have brought endless invention to their task of decorative embellishment.

Fabergé Dealers and Collectors

COLLECTING Fabergé pieces began with Fabergé's first sale, but re-sales, trading, and changes in collectors broadened after the Russian Revolution with the movement of Russian refugees and émigrés to Europe, Asia, and America.

Though the changing of hands of and interest in these art items have continued to the present, there was not much demand for Fabergé in the 1920s and '30s. These pieces were looked at as souvenirs of a bygone Victorian era or secondhand bric-a-brac, and sold for very little. Wartski pioneered transporting and selling Fabergé pieces, and A La Vieille Russie has been a distinguished dealer in Fabergé items since the 1930s as well.

In the 1930s American dealer Armand Hammer, who bought, sold, and traded Russian goods, reintroduced Fabergé to America in a unique way. He bought art, jewelry, and antiques from the Antiquariat (a division of the Soviet Foreign Trade Commission) and then began selling "Czarist treasures" and "art of the Czars" in popular department stores throughout the United States. Hammer actually rekindled interest in Czarist Russia by using public relations techniques in his promotion and often giving lectures about Russia. Hammer started his sales with the fabulous eggs in 1931. When he got to Palm Beach (with his store on Worth Avenue), he promoted the imperial image with a cigarette case "certified," according to him, to have been the Czar's. Even price tags were made with the double-headed eagle crest of the imperial family. This indeed prompted people to buy more than a piece of history. Hammer Gallery pieces have ended up in some of the best collections; it is to be hoped that not all were identified as a treasure from the Czar's apartment.

Dealers in Russian art, jewelry, antiques, and gold and silver items have done much to keep this period of Russian history alive. While the Soviet government was de-acquisitioning art and antiques—melting gold and silver pieces into ingots and extracting gems from jewelers' art to sell, dealers were collecting. By doing so, they were recording those items for reference, promoting Fabergé, and selling the taste of prerevolutionary Russia.

Additionally, many of the auction houses have kept the interest in Russian art and Fabergé alive by offering good color catalogues and photography. They are the middlemen between the buyer and the seller, providing information and provenance about each piece. Gerard Hill of Sotheby's and Alexis de Tiesenhausen of Christie's have become experts in producing these informative catalogues which are books in themselves on Fabergé, his art, and his cases. Collectors eagerly await the next sale catalogue and pore over the splashy color photographs to see which new piece might augment their collection. Then the bidding wars begin, and the pieces go to their new owners, adding yet another layer of provenance.

The public's interest in a certain style of art, jewelry, or a certain artist such as Fabergé is often gauged by how well a particular auction does; many collectors watch the results just as investors watch the stock market. Were all of the items sold, did they fetch the prices anticipated, did the prices far exceed those expected (such as at the Duchess of Windsor sale), or sadly, has the public's enthusiasm diminished? Sometimes the results are even reported in the next day's news.

This world of Fabergé dealers, purveyors, and auction establishments is a tight-knit group of Fabergé experts, quasi experts, and historians. They all know each other, they see each other at many of the same sales and exhibitions, and vie for the business of some of the same collectors. Most important, they all agree on the same basic principles of the touch, feel, and technical perfection of Fabergé pieces. They sometimes do not agree on the authenticity of a case, no matter how distinct the hallmarks might be, asking, "Is it right?" (when a layperson might wonder, is it "real" or "fake?"). This group has acquired its expertise through years of buying, selling, and handling Fabergé, and the mistakes they make are fewer and fewer.

Following are some interesting thoughts on cases from a number of these experts who are in today's world of Fabergé.

A. Kenneth Snowman
Chairman, Wartski, London

I SHARE John Traina's enthusiasm for the design and manufacture of Fabergé's cigarette cases. The cases themselves are justifiably regarded as relatively uncharted territory, although I have already written on this subject in some detail in my books on Fabergé.

My maternal grandfather, Morris Wartski, joined the family business founded in 1865. Then my late father, Emanuel Snowman, became involved and opened a London branch of Wartski in 1911 at 13 New Bond Street. Several moves were made before the firm arrived at 138 Regent Street in 1929, where we functioned happily until he died in 1970. In 1975 we moved to our present nest in Grafton Street, a turning off Bond Street, since in the view of my colleagues and myself, Regent Street had become less interesting for our sort of business.

From the days of Edward VII, my father personally enjoyed the patronage of the royal family. But perhaps the most significant work of his life was the unflagging determination he applied in the 1930s to rescuing Jews from Nazi Germany.

In 1925 my father learned that the Soviets had confiscated all the treasure they could lay their hands on from the aristocracy and the rich and had created something they called the Antiquariat, involving the Kremlin Museum and the Hermitage. They were now proposing to offer for sale these treasures, which they had noisily despised as playthings for the rich—precisely what Fabergé had in mind when he had his objects made. My father was the first courageous pioneer to venture forth to the Soviet Union from Europe and thereafter made annual pilgrimages until 1939, bringing back quantities of fabulous objects made in the seventeenth and eighteenth centuries, in addition to numerous works by Fabergé, including no fewer than eleven of the imperial Easter eggs.

I decided to join the firm in 1940. In 1954 it was decreed that my wife, Sallie, and I should attend the sales at the Koubbeh Palace in Cairo, where King Farouk's accumulated goodies were to be auctioned. This was an exciting event and we were able to acquire many remarkable items, mainly eighteenth-century goldsmith's work, jewels, and objects by Fabergé.

Our small firm, never more than about six people (plus a porter and a driver), has attracted some extremely fascinating characters over the years: collectors with their own ideas, glamorous theater people, and scholars from the museums. The late Malcolm Forbes told me in Moscow just a few weeks before he died that he had acquired his very first Fabergé item—a gold cigarette case—after spotting it in our Regent Street window. It marked the start of the distinguished collection so beautifully displayed by his family in New York; we have been privileged to contribute to it over the years, with many items including the Lilies of the Valley and Coronation eggs which my father had bought in Russia. I remember well how Noël Coward used to enjoy strolling into Regent Street and gossiping in the most entertaining way. Bing Crosby and, later, Frank Sinatra visited us when they were in London, as did Simone Signoret and Yves Montand, Lauren Bacall, and Ingrid Bergman, to mention just a few. Fred Zinnemann, king of filmmakers, was a great charmer and friend and is deeply missed.

The English stage and entertainment and music worlds have been well represented from the time of Henry Ainley, and I am happy to report that this tradition has been well maintained by such distinguished names as Gielgud and Olivier and, never forgetting the now much-missed Music Hall tradition, marvelous Bud Flanagan. We have been honored by the direct patronage of kingdoms abroad and of our own royal family in the most generous fashion. In a world fast declining in so many ways, we in our land count ourselves singularly blessed with our caring royalty.

In 1977 we put on an exhibition of Fabergé at the Victoria and Albert Museum, which included a large part of the Royal Collection. Thanks to the generosity of Her Majesty, the enthusiasm of Sir Roy Strong, and my own stipulation that there should be no committee to frustrate our arrangements, it turned out to be, according to the V & A, the most successful exhibition the museum has ever put on, with long queues winding round the building waiting to get inside. Possibly as a result of all this, I was asked to arrange and prepare the catalogue for a show for New York's Cooper-Hewitt Museum, the Smithsonian Institution's National Museum of Design, in 1983 entitled "Fabergé, Jeweler to Royalty."

In 1986 something happened that represented, for me, some sort of poetic justice. A gentleman got in touch with me from America and said that he and his sister owned two books of designs by Fabergé and would I be interested in seeing and possibly acquiring them? When, some weeks later, I saw what was put in front of me, I could scarcely believe my eyes. These were no sketchbooks, as that term is understood: they were, believe it or not, the stockbooks of the Holmström workshops. (Holmström was one of Fabergé's chief workmasters at the time.)

Every item produced from March 6, 1909, to March 20, 1915, was specified in detail: a skillfully expressed watercolor drawing of each jewel or object appeared on the left side of every page and a highly detailed description, beautifully written by hand, spread across the rest. We acquired these marvelous authentic documentary volumes with a feeling of enormous gratitude toward Osvald K. Jurison, a thirty-three-year-old diamond setter who worked for Holmström. When the firm was closed down by the Soviets, Jurison had the wisdom to rescue the books and escape with them to Latvia in 1935. His son and daughter in the States made it possible for us to acquire them.

ALEXANDER VON SOLODKOFF
Ermitage Ltd., London

CZAR NICHOLAS II was a keen smoker, and, what is more in the context of this book, he liked to keep his cigarettes in appropriately beautiful etuis, or cases. This apparently initiated the idea for his mother, the Dowager Empress Marie Feodorovna, to give him as presents cigarette cases made by the famous court jewelers of St. Petersburg, especially by Fabergé. There were three occasions for presents during the year: the Czar's birthday (May 6), his patron saint's day of St. Nicholas (December 6), and Christmas. In all three instances the Empress regularly chose ever more beautiful, elaborate, and elegant cases as presents for her son. They were all engraved inside the cover, and sometimes also inside the base with a presentation inscription copied from an autograph, a handwritten dedication by the Empress. Usually it read in Russian script, "To dear Nicky, from Mama," together with the date or the Russian word used in the family for Christmas—*yolka*, meaning Christmas tree. The wording of the presentation phrase was not always the same; it would include variations on the Russian word for "dear," "beloved," or "darling."

On his thirty-second birthday, in 1900, the Czar was given a cigarette case of pale green enamel on sunburst *guilloché* ground decorated with a clover set with four large diamonds (see p. 50). Acquired through Ermitage Ltd., this case is signed by Fabergé and his workmaster August Hollming. It is interesting to note that 1900 was the year of the Paris Exposition Universelle, where Carl Fabergé and his firm were praised in highest terms.

DR. FABIAN STEIN
Ermitage Ltd., London

FOR FIVE HUNDRED YEARS, since Columbus's men observed native Cubans "drinking" smoke from leaves that had been dried, rolled, and burned, tobacco has played a significant role in social history. No jeweler in the late nineteenth and early twentieth centuries illustrates this point as well as Fabergé. A glance into the sales ledgers of Fabergé's London branch shows how important a place cigarette cases held among his luxury items. Hardly a week went by without the sale of one, two, or more such cases. Often one buyer would purchase several at a time, obviously intending them as presents.

In total, 420 cigarette cases were sold through the London branch of Fabergé between October 1907 and June 1912, and it may be interesting to note that 170 of these—40 percent—went to women buyers. However, the gallantry of this bygone age seems epitomized by a small lady's cigarette case, presented and engraved by an admirer with the dedication: "Je voudrais être cigarette pour habiter un instant vos lèvres et puis m'éteindre" (see p. 142).

Mark Schaffer

A La Vieille Russie, New York

CIGARETTE CASES, by the very nature of their use, require an intimate, tactile relationship with the user, who is afforded that pleasure of touching that we in the decorative arts enjoy so much. They are the sum total of many art forms brought together in a small package. Of such small objects—in which we have been dealing since our founding in Kiev in 1851—Fabergé was a master, and each case is a joy to touch. The moment I receive any piece, I roll it around in my hands and might even close my eyes for a full experience. I execute this ritual not only for the very pleasure, but also in search of Fabergé's hand. In this realm of the tactile, John Traina's choices shine.

I'm immediately reminded of one of his early purchases. This engine-turned gold presentation case, set with inscription and dates in diamonds, boasts a deep texture pleasing to even the roughest of hands. The case is wider than most, providing a great canvas for the name "Elizaveta" (sister of Alexandra Feodorovna), splayed out against a frame of acanthus leaves and multiple colors of gold (see p. 67). Another gold case of similarly unusual shape is Mr. Traina's cigarette case in the form of a cane handle, neatly topped with a carnelian. This columnar case's swirled form disguises its true identity, and, as a cane handle, is meant to be held in the hand. The hinge runs the width of the case (see p. 142).

Shape, even for cigarette cases, thus varies, and one of the most pleasing in Fabergé's repertoire is the tubular case. In Mr. Traina's collection is one he purchased from us, of spectacular yet subtle mauve color over a *guilloché* ground (see p. 74). If there was ever a piece that felt like Fabergé, this would be it.

Mauve is a demure color, however. Imperial or royal blue is not—one can see it from across the room! I'm now thinking of Mr. Traina's richly, deeply colored *guilloché* imperial presentation case of traditional square-cornered shape by Hollming, the cover set with a diamond-set double-headed imperial eagle (see p. 93).

Mr. Traina's extra-thick blue *guilloché* enamel case has a strong Louis XV rococo character. The scrolls, though deeply chiseled, are wonderfully smooth (see p. 109). But many cases have no immediately obvious source. For example, especially creative is Mr. Traina's purple *guilloché* enamel case, with overlaid diamond-set gold laurel swags, opaque white enamel zigzag trellis, and Greek key border (see p. 72). Here again, its design is visible to the touch and screams Fabergé.

One feature of Fabergé's work that particularly interests me is the use of a wide variety of materials, and cigarette cases certainly exemplify this characteristic. At one extreme are wooden cases, of which Mr. Traina has collected from us both tubular and rectangular examples in palisander (see pp. 130–31). In each case, the well-carved and smoothly burnished wood offers a beautifully delicate sensation to the hand. In stark contrast, his gold-mounted gunmetal or steel cigarette case can be icy to the touch. But its highly polished surface renders the piece sensuous (see p. 67). Moreover, the gold-framed cigarette compartment and separate match compartment fit so snugly that, without looking, one would almost believe that the box did not open at all!

ULLA TILLANDER-GODENHIELM
A. Tillander, Helsinki

THE CIGARETTE CASE was no doubt Fabergé's most successful article in terms of sales and popularity. The production of this popular object did not slacken even during World War I and the difficult years that followed. Jalmari Haikonen, Finnish-born engraver at Henrik Wigström's workshop (1915–18) gives us his personal description of how a multiplicity of etuis passed through the production line: "In our engravers' row there were at times up to forty cases in line waiting for the next stage of work to be done. One man worked the *guilloché* machine, we engravers repaired and corrected the slips of the machine. The polishers put the finishing touch to the cases by hand."

Many of the cigarette cases handled by this enthusiastic young engraver and his colleagues are now part of John Traina's magnificent collection.

With the help of the recently discovered sketch album from the workshop of Henrik Wigström we are in fact able to draw some conclusions as to which type of cigarette case was à la mode during what may have been the two most prosperous years of the House of Fabergé. The album contains sketches of 155 different models of cigarette cases designed and sold during the years 1911 and 1912.

One can detect a definite trend in the design of cigarette cases for these two years, which points toward a shaking off of the past. The design of cigarette cases, so closely linked to the haute couture of the day, heralds a change in taste. The gold cigarette case (see p. 139) in the Traina Collection is an example of this gradual change in taste. This particular case, though still retaining an engine-turned decor and laurel-leaf bands, is an important step toward the quintessence of simplicity. One could also comment that the pushpiece, either the diminutive arc set with rose-cut diamonds, or the simple setting with a gem cut *en cabochon*, is not changed. This small element of function stubbornly remains the same and almost serves as a trademark of Fabergé.

Two cases in the Traina Collection (see pp. 127 and 142) represent the height of fashion in 1911–12. These cases have the simple effect of alternating bands of narrow and wide stripes and stripes of two or three colors of gold. From our present vantage point, these designs may not appear striking, but at the beginning of our century they were very avant-garde.

The ladies' cases are, in general, more embellished than the men's. The *en plein* enameled decor on an engine-turned surface remains in fashion. Pink is the predominant color in enameling during these two years. The ladies' cases are usually much smaller than those of the gentlemen and so slim that the element of function seems to have been overlooked. There are quite a few cases with an oval section opening at the top, an ingenious form with a slim outline with space inside for many cigarettes. The Traina Collection contains fine examples of this type.

There are also a number of cylindrical cigarette cases (see p. 133), which at one end hold a mouthpiece. The cylinder case looks very attractive on a dinner table next to its owner.

Hardstone cases are classics in Fabergé's production. In 1911–12 they were still the fashion for evening wear. The mottled pine green Siberian nephrite is by far the most popular hardstone. The Traina Collection has many fine examples of these elegant cases. The cases shown on page 113 are a ladies' trunk-shaped box with jeweled clasp and hinges, and a man's nephrite case with an enameled and jeweled band following the outline of the lid.

ANDRE RUZHNIKOV
Private dealer/collector
Palo Alto, California

FOR FUTURE COLLECTORS, my advice is to buy what you can afford. If you can't afford it, don't dare buy it. Try to hook up with someone you trust to guide you—someone established and knowledgeable, someone with a track record and experience. Many people buy and sell Fabergé, and there are plenty of quasi experts. Since Fabergé has attained a great deal of value, all sorts of personalities have jumped into the fray of dealing in Fabergé. These newcomers cannot possibly have the knowledge that can only be gained through years of experience. As a native Russian with twenty-five years working in this area, I have made my mistakes and learned from them. This sort of knowlege would be worth a great deal to a collector of today.

I would not recommend that anyone buy a Fabergé piece, particularly a pricey one, from somebody who serendipitously stumbled upon it. In most cases serendipity leads to nothing but losses. There are no secrets in this trade.

To talk about Fabergé fakes is to open a Pandora's box; every area is fraught with danger. Given the many styles of Fabergé, some fraudulent dealers buy a piece of silver for very little money and stamp it "Fabergé." Very often it then passes through lesser-known auction houses and into the hands of ignorant collectors.

For private collectors—of cigarette cases or other items—the best advice is to buy the best from the best. But be careful: The best appear to be increasingly hard to find.

Workmasters in the Collection

Where information is known, workmasters represented in the collection are as follows. Others are known by a name or initial only, as listed in the captions.

Head Workmasters, St. Petersburg

KOLLIN, ERIK AUGUST (1836–1901)
First head workmaster, 1872–86
Part of Fabergé's Scandinavian workforce
High-quality goldsmith work, specializing in gold and filigree
Worked for Holmström before becoming head workmaster

PERCHIN, MICHAEL EVLAMPIEVICH (1860–1903)
Head workmaster after Kollin, 1886–1903
Used rococo style and rocaille elements
Of Russian peasant stock
FABERGÉ in Cyrillic with no other workmaster's initials sometimes indicates case was made in the Perchin workshop (as with Wigström)
Imperial Easter eggs were created in his workshop

WIGSTRÖM, HENRIK EMANUEL (1862–1923)
Perchin's assistant from 1886
Head workmaster after Perchin's death in 1903
Became responsible for the imperial Easter eggs after Perchin's death
Objects often similar to Perchin's Louis XVI and Empire styles
Known for highest standards of workmanship
Part of Fabergé's Swedish-Finn workforce
Many articles bear his signature due to Fabergé's increased business
FABERGÉ in Cyrillic with no other workmaster's initials sometimes indicates case was made in this workshop (as with Perchin)

Other Fabergé Workmasters

AARNE, JOHAN VIKTOR (1863–1934)
Of Finnish origin
In the Fabergé firm 1891–1904
Worked in gold, silver, and enamel

AFANASSIEV, FEODOR
Of Russian origin
High-quality articles, including cigarette cases

ARMFELT, KARL GUSTAV HJALMAR (1873–1959)
A Swedish-Finn
Known for articles of high quality in hard stones and enameled gold and silver
Worked for Fabergé under the direction of Nevalainen, 1895–1904
After buying his own workshop, continued to supply Fabergé until 1916

GORIANOV, ANDREI
Specializing in gold cigarette cases, he was an occasional supplier to Fabergé
Took over Reimer's workshop after his death

HOLLMING, AUGUST FREDERIK (1854–1913)
A Finn
Specialized in gold, stone, and enamel pieces
Made many cigarette cases, including fine examples in enamel

HOLMSTRÖM, ALBERT WOLDEMAR (1876–1925)

Took over his father's workshop in 1903 and continued to use his AH hallmark

Made cigarette cases

Famous pieces include the Mosaic and Winter eggs

HOLMSTRÖM, AUGUST WILHELM (1829–1903)

Part of Fabergé's Swedish-Finn workforce

In 1857 became Fabergé's head jeweler

Made cigarette cases

Famous for Lilies of the Valley basket and imperial crown miniature replicas

LUNDELL, KARL GUSTAV JOHANSSON (1833–1906)

Part of Fabergé's Swedish-Finn workforce

Worked in Fabergé's Odessa branch, specializing in cigarette cases

MICKELSON, ANDERS (1839–1913)

Part of Fabergé's Swedish-Finn workforce

Made gold cigarette cases and small enameled objects

Produced articles in St. Petersburg

Along with Ringe's widow and Soloviev, he took over Ringe's workshop after his death

NEVALAINEN, ANDERS JOHANSSON (1858–1933)

Part of Fabergé's Finnish workforce

Became workmaster for Fabergé under Holmström in 1885

Made enameled cigarette cases in gold or silver

Occasionally produced items for the Moscow branch as well

NIUKKANEN, GABRIEL ZACHARIASSON

A Finn

Worked from 1898–1912 in his independent workshop

Known for his work in gold and silver cigarette cases

Managed Fabergé's Odessa workshop for a time

PIHL, KNUT OSKAR (1860–1897)

Between 1887 and 1897 he was the head goldsmith in Fabergé's Moscow branch

Apprenticed with August Holmström, as did his son Oskar Woldemar

His daughter, Alma Theresia, designed the Winter Egg and other snowflake designs

RAPPOPORT, JULIUS ALEKSANDROVICH (1864–1916)

Of German-Jewish origin

Was Fabergé's head silversmith and began working for Fabergé in 1883

Had his own independent workshop, even after Fabergé's move to Bolshaya Morskaya

His hallmarks can also be found on pieces with the Moscow mark

REIMER, WILHELM (d. ca. 1898)

Made enamel and gold objects

RINGE, PHILIPP THEODOR

Of German descent

Had his own workshop beginning in 1893

Supplied small objects in enameled gold or silver to Fabergé

RÜCKERT, FEODOR

Of German descent, born and worked in Moscow

Had the only cloisonné enamel workshop

Supplied Fabergé and others beginning in 1877

SCHRAMM, EDUARD WILHELM

Of German descent, born in St. Petersburg

Supplied Fabergé with cigarette cases and gold objects before 1899

SOLOVIEV, VLADIMIR

Known for enameled silver

Often associated with enameled pieces intended for export to London; his mark usually found under the enamel

THIELEMANN, ALFRED

Of German descent, born in St. Petersburg

Master from 1858

Produced small pieces of jewelry and objects

His son, Karl Rudolph, took his place after his death

Hallmark similar to those of Tillander, Tobinkov, and Treiden

WÄKEVA, ALEXANDER (1870–1957)

Headed his father's workshop from 1910–17

Also made silver pieces

WÄKEVA, STEPHAN (1833–1910)

Finnish workmaster beginning in 1856

Supplied Fabergé with articles of silver

Some Fabergé competitors found in this collection

ADLER, ANDRE KARLOVICH

Well-known St. Petersburg gold- and silversmith

Owned Adler & Co.

Produced orders, decorations, and miscellaneous objects

Work is represented in the collection of the State Historical Museum, Moscow

Marks formerly considered to be those of "Astreyden & Co.," whose existence has recently been disproved

ARNDT, SAMUEL

St. Petersburg, active between 1845 and 1890

Produced small objects in silver, gold, and enamel

BRAGIN, ANDREI

St. Petersburg, beginning in 1880

Produced gold cigarette cases

BRITZIN, IVAN SAVELEVITCH

St. Petersburg workshop

Produced, among other objects, cigarette cases in *guilloché* enamel

Occasional supplier to Fabergé

His work exported to Britain
and the U. S., 1900–17

GRACHEV, GAVRIL PETROVITCH
St. Petersburg, 1866–73; then his
sons took over, naming the
firm Grachev Brothers
Specialized in the production of
silver and samorodok cigarette
cases
Named Court Jeweler in 1896

HAHN, KARL KARLOWITCH
St. Petersburg, around 1880
One of Fabergé's main competitors in imperial presentation
boxes
Produced jeweled enamel boxes
in the Fabergé style

KHLEBNIKOV, IVAN PETROVITCH
St. Petersburg in 1867–70;
Moscow, beginning in 1871
Produced gold and silver ciga-
rette cases
Awarded the imperial warrant in
1882
Also known for Russian-style
enamels in cloisonné and
plique-à-jour

KOECHLI, FRIEDRICH
St. Petersburg, 1874
Specialized in gold presentation
cigarette cases

KUZMICHEV, ANTIP IVANOVITCH
Moscow
Specialized in gold and
samorodok cigarette cases

LORIE, FEDOR ANATOLEVITCH
Moscow, 1871–1917
Specialized in gold cigarette
cases

MARSHAK, JOSIF ABRAMOVITCH
Kiev, 1878–1917
Goldsmith producing gold
and samorodok cigarette
cases

MOROZOV, IVAN YEVDOKIMOVITCH
St. Petersburg, 1849–1917
Produced many articles, includ-
ing cigarette cases

MOSCOW SOCIETY OF JEWELERS
Limited society of Moscow goldsmith artels*

NICHOLS & PLINCKE
Owned The English Shop, a
high-quality silversmith shop
in St. Petersburg, located on
Bolshaya Morskaya, near
Fabergé's studio

PISKARYEV, ALEXANDER IVANOVICH
Moscow workshop, 1908–13
Numerous objects in the collec-
tion of the State Historical
Museum, Moscow

ROSEN, JAKOV MIKHAILOVITCH
St. Petersburg, 1900–17
Specialized in cigarette cases

SALTIKOV, IVAN
Moscow workshop
Occasionally supplied cloisonné
objects to Fabergé

TILLANDER, ALEXANDER EDWARD
St. Petersburg, 1870–1917;
Helsinki, 1917
Workshop produced many
objects, including cigarette
cases

Additionally, Fabergé's
St. Petersburg staff included many
designers, miniaturists—including
court painter VASSILI ZUIEV—and
modelers, together with a large
number of ordinary craftsmen.
Something like twenty craftsmen
were employed just to make the fitted outer wooden boxes for the
individual pieces.

———————

* Independent cooperatives of
workmasters, jewelers, and gold-
and silversmiths in Moscow and
St. Petersburg beginning around
1896.

Acknowledgments

I would like to express my sincere gratitude to some of the people who graciously devoted their time, energy, expertise, or support during the creation of this book. Special thanks go to Fred Lyon (photographer), Elizabeth Whelan Roman (research director), Mitchell Shenker (photography), Archduke Géza von Habsburg, Mikhail Piotrovsky, and Danielle Steel. In addition, I am grateful to:

Mary Ann Allin
Edward Asprey
Sharon AvRutick
Susan Badder
Bernard Barryte
Albert Bartridge Jr.
Irina Roublon Belotelkin
Kate Brooks
Ruth Buchanan
Nicola Bulgari
Butterfield's
Bess Cadwell
Margaret R. Chace
William Chaney
Therese Chen
Christie's
Barnaby Conrad III
Jack Cowart
Charles Crederoli
Simon Critchell
David Park Curry
Elena S. Danielson, Ph.D.
Christian de Guigne IV
Helene de Ludinghausen
Alexis de Tiesenhausen
Gretchen DeWitt
Jim Dobson
Tatiana Fabergé
Christopher Forbes
Gordon Getty
Karin Godenhielm
Paul Gottlieb

Olle Granath
Mrs. Carl Hahn
Henry Hawley
Valery Heifitz
Stefan Hemmerle
Gerard Hill
Alice Milica Ilich
Doug Inglish
John Webster Keefe
Laura Knoop King
Fred Leighton
Dr. Marina N. Lopato
Dirk Luykx
Christel Ludewig McCanless
Mikhail Y. Medvedev
Lee Hunt Miller
Geoffrey Munn
Tatiana Muntian
William E. Murray
Steven A. Nash
Riitta Niskanen
Anne Odom
Bernard Osher
Harry S. Parker III
Irina Polynina
Jeff Post
Lynette G. Proler
Katherine Purcell
Joyce Lasky Reed
Donald Rees
Hugh Roberts
Stan G. Roman

Prince Nikita Romanov
Lucky Roosevelt
Andre Ruzhnikov
Teresa Safon
Mark A. Schaffer
Paul Schaffer
Peter L. Schaffer
Valentin V. Skurlov
Sara Slavin
Galina G. Smorodinova
A. Kenneth Snowman
Sotheby's
Dr. Fabian Stein
Marilyn Pfeifer Swezey
Ulla Tillander-Godenhielm
Todd Traina
Trevor Traina
Margaret Kelly Trombly
Robyn Tromeur
Andrea L. Van de Kamp
Kirsten Verdi
Amy L. Vinchesi
Prinzessin von Sachsen
Alexander von Solodkoff
Richard Walker
Christopher English Walling
Elsebeth Welander-Berggren
Martha West
Harold Whitbeck
Heather White
Jennifer Ziegler

Selected Bibliography

Books

Bainbridge, H. C. *Peter Carl Fabergé: His Life and Work 1846–1920.* London, B. T. Batsford, Ltd., 1949

Belyakova, Zoia. *The Romanov Legacy: The Palaces of St. Petersburg.* London, Hazar Publishing, Ltd., 1994

Breitling, Gunter, et al. *Gold.* New York, Alpine Fine Arts Collection, Ltd., 1981

Cerwinske, Laura. *Russian Imperial Style.* New York, Prentice-Hall, 1990

Curry, David Park. *Fabergé.* Richmond, Virginia Museum of Fine Arts, 1995

Custine, Marquis de. *Empire of the Czar: A Journey Through Eternal Russia.* New York, Doubleday, 1989

Epstein, Edward Jay. *Dossier: The Secret History of Armand Hammer.* New York, Random House, 1996

Fabergé, Tatiana, et al. *The Fabergé Imperial Easter Eggs.* London, Christie, Manson and Woods, Ltd., 1997

Galitzine, Prince George. *Imperial Splendour: Palaces and Monasteries of Old Russia.* New York, Penguin, 1991

Ghosn, Michel Y. *Objets de vertu par Fabergé.* Editions Dar An-Nahar

Habsburg, Géza von. *Fabergé in America.* New York, Thames and Hudson; San Francisco, Fine Arts Museums of San Francisco, 1996

Habsburg-Lothringen, G. von, and A. von Solodkoff. *Fabergé: Court Jeweler to the Tsars.* New York, Rizzoli, 1979

Hawley, Henry. *Fabergé and His Contemporaries: The India Early Minshall Collection of The Cleveland Museum of Art.* Cleveland, The Cleveland Museum of Art, 1967

Hill, Gerard, G. G. Smorodinova, and B. L. Ulyanova. *Fabergé and the Russian Master Goldsmiths.* New York, Hugh Lauter Levin, 1989

Iroshnikov, Mikhail P., Yury B. Shelayev, and Liudmila A. Protsai. *Before the Revolution: St. Petersburg in Photographs: 1890–1914.* New York, Harry N. Abrams, Inc., 1991

Keefe, John Webster. *Masterpieces of Fabergé: The Matilda Geddings Gray Foundation Collection.* New Orleans, New Orleans Museum of Art, 1993

Kelly, Margaret. *Imperial Surprises.* New York, Harry N. Abrams, Inc., 1994

Kirichenko, Eugenia. *The Russian Style.* London, Laurence King, 1991

Kurth, Peter. *Tsar: The Lost World of Nicholas and Alexandra.* Toronto, Little, Brown and Company, 1995

Massie, Robert K. *The Romanovs: The Final Chapter.* New York, Ballantine, 1995

Massie, Suzanne. *Pavlovsk: The Life of a Russian Palace.* Boston, Little, Brown and Company, 1990

McCanless, Christel Ludewig. *Fabergé and His Works: An Annotated Bibliography of the First Century of His Art.* Metuchen, N.J., The Scarecrow Press, 1994

Milner, John. *A Dictionary of Russian and Soviet Artists 1420–1970.* Woodbridge, Antique Collector's Club, 1993

Odom, Anne. *Russian Enamels: Kievan Rus to Fabergé.* London, Philip Wilson, 1996

Pfeffer, Susanna. *Fabergé Eggs: Masterpieces from Czarist Russia.* New York, Hugh Lauter Levin, 1990

Postnikova-Losseva, M. M., N. G. Platonova, and B. L. Ulianova. *L'Orfevrerie et la Bijouterie au XV–XX ss. (Territoire de l'URSS).* Moscow, Edition Unves, 1995

Radzinsky, Edvard. *The Last Tsar: The Life and Death of Nicholas II.* New York, Doubleday, 1992

Raymer, Steve. *St. Petersburg.* Atlanta, Turner Publishing, 1994

Rodimzeva, Irina, Nikolai Rachmanov, and Alfons Raimann. *The Kremlin and Its Treaures.* New York, Rizzoli, 1987

Snowman, A. Kenneth. *The Art of Carl Fabergé.* London, Faber and Faber, 1953

———. *Carl Fabergé: Goldsmith to the Imperial Court of Russia.* New York, Greenwich House, 1983

———. *Fabergé Lost and Found: The Recently Discovered Jewelry Designs from the St. Petersburg Archives.* New York, Harry N. Abrams, Inc., 1993

Solodkoff, Alexander von. *The Art of Carl Fabergé.* New York, Crown, 1988

———. *Masterpieces from the House of Fabergé.* New York, Harry N. Abrams, Inc., 1984

Waterfield, Hermione, and Christopher Forbes. *Fabergé: Imperial Eggs and Other Fantasies.* New York, Bramhall House, 1980

Exhibitions and Catalogues

"Fabergé," Bavarian National Museum, Munich, Germany, 1987

"Fabergé: Fabergé from the Royal Collection," The Queen's Gallery, Buckingham Palace, London, England, 1995

"Carl Fabergé: Goldsmith to the Tsar," Nationalmuseum, Stockholm, Sweden, 1997

"Fabergé, Goldsmith to the Imperial Court," M. H. de Young Memorial Museum, San Francisco, California, 1964

"Fabergé: The Imperial Eggs," San Diego Museum of Art, San Diego, California, 1989

"Fabergé: Imperial Jeweller," State Hermitage Museum, St. Petersburg; Musée des Arts Décoratifs, Paris; Victoria and Albert Museum, London, 1993

"Fabergé, Jeweler to Royalty, From the Collection of Her Majesty Queen Elizabeth II and Other British Lenders," Cooper-Hewitt Museum, New York, 1983

"Fabergé: Juwelier des Zarenhofes," Hamburg Museum of Art, Hamburg, Germany, 1995

"Fabergé: A Loan Exhibition for the Benefit of the Cooper-Hewitt Museum," A La Vieille Russie, New York, 1983

"Fabergé: Loistavaa Kultasepäntaidetta," Lahti Art Museum, Lahti, Finland, 1997

"Fabergé and Finland: Exquisite Objects," Corcoran Gallery of Art, Washington, D.C., 1996–97

"Fabergé in America," The Metropolitan Museum of Art, New York; M. H. de Young Memorial Museum, Fine Arts Museums of San Francisco; Virginia Museum of Fine Arts, Richmond; New Orleans Museum of Art, New Orleans; The Cleveland Museum of Art, Cleveland, 1996–97

"The Fabulous Epoch of Fabergé," Catherine Palace in Tsarskoye Selo, St. Petersburg; Paris, France; Moscow, 1992

"Great Fabergé in the Hermitage," State Hermitage Museum, St. Petersburg, 1997–98

Christie's and Sotheby's Fabergé sales catalogues, 1974–97

Index